TALK IT OUT!
4 Steps to Managing People Problems in Your Organization

Dr. Daniel Dana

First Edition, First Printing, December 1989

Library of Congress Cataloging in Publication Data

International Standard Book No. 0-87425-122-2

ACKNOWLEDGMENTS

For their conceptual and editorial suggestions at various stages in the preparation of the manuscript, I am indebted to Patricia Barone, Stefan Berg, Ellen Dolsen, Linda Pleau Duffy, Barbara Durham, Tom Fiutak, Paula Flynn, Virginia Foley, Ron Heilmann, Roger Herrick, Connie Holmes, Jean Johnson, Vivian Kotler, Ellie Linden, Gay Lustig, Ruthanne Marchetti, John Ogilvie, Darrel Ray, Mindy Rosenberg, Bob Schachat, Mike Schulde, Mary Ann Schwartz, George Scurlock, Elaine Stuart, Carolyn Tertes, Wallace Wilkins, and Jim Wolf.

I extend my appreciation to the following associates of ODT, Inc. for their helpful comments on cultural diversity: Bob Abramms, Carmen Colin, Gil Gonzalez, Diane Johns, Hank Karp, Diane LaMountain, and George Simons.

Finally, I wish to thank Chris Hunter of Human Resource Development Press for championing this book.

To
Susan
may her life be richly blessed
with well-managed differences

CONTENTS

Part 1:   THE CHALLENGE

Part 2:   THE 4-STEP METHOD

LIST OF FIGURES

FOREWORD:

Toward All of Us Doing Better with Conflict

Ask any executive or manager how much time he or she spends in dealing with conflicts—before, during, and after—and you will get a range of estimates. But *all* of those estimates will be high: they will account for substantial proportions of even the extended workdays common in today's industry and government.

For years, I asked that question of the many managers and executives I encountered—as consultant, educator, facilitator, administrator, researcher, and friend. I recall few estimates lower than 15-20 percent; and I have a firm recollection of numerous estimates at the 50% level or above.

My own direct management experiences relate to economic times when everything was coming up roses, and the basic challenge to many then was to spend quick, with only secondary attention to spending wisely and well. Even so, perhaps a quarter of my management time went to dealing with conflict, both as a participant and facilitator for other participants. And, at least in my view of myself, I was the determined confronter who tried to unearth difficulties early and who believed in getting to problem-situations when they were still local irritations. Many administrators, I find, would rather follow our laconic President Coolidge, who advised: "If you see 10 problems coming down the track, just wait, and 9 will soon be gone." Perhaps, but that tenth one might be a lulu. And Coolidge had no good advice for those problems which did not die on their own.

Think of what those estimates of conflict in organizations imply, even if one discounts them by a quarter, or even a half. They represent huge amounts of time and emotional energy spent gearing-up for conflict, acting it out, or trying to manage its multiple consequences.

Conflict-avoiders have little to recommend them, but the proverbial bull-in-the-china-shop is worse still. Perhaps there is no sadder situation than avowed conflict-resolvers with such inept skills and attitudes that they create additional turmoil in the process of trying to deal with whatever conflict exists, or of exercising prescient anticipation about the conflict that is just about to surface.

The potential for conflict in organizations looms large. Nobody should have to draw elaborate pictures, then, about the timely salience of Dr. Daniel Dana's *TALK IT OUT! 4 Steps to Managing People Problems in Your Organization.* This is clearly a book about our times, and for our times. Dan Dana's book sheds penetrating light on what can be the wasted heat of conflict, if avoided or bumbled into.

Let me suggest a few senses in which *TALK IT OUT!* has much to recommend it—if only from my perspective, and at the risk of gilding Dan's lily. The book:

- represents one of a short list of titles that combine the why and the how—theory as well as guides for direct application

- presents an approach that has been tested in a range of contexts

- rests on values that I cherish: it is not one of those glib lightweight popularizations which propose to tell you how to do it to the other person before it gets done to you, while

providing unctuous pseudo-reassurance that you will feel
good in that doing to others

- works at dealing *with* conflict, rather than trying to finesse it
  or promising some easy inoculation against its consequences

- will be useful in action as well as in learning situations—in
  academic coursework, as well as in-service training in both
  business and government

Two other major features of *TALK IT OUT!* also deserve emphasis, I judge. First, the book will appeal to the specialist, but it is
written for all of us who spend the bulk of our working lives in and
around organizations and groups. There will be occasions when
specialists need to be called to help in dealing with conflicting situations, Dana correctly urges, but life will be far simpler for all of us
if we do more of it on our own. If nothing else, people tend to "save
up" issues for specialists, if they are regularly available, and that
may occasion costly delays and distortion of situations better handled as they occurred. Dana provides very useful guidance for all of
us—for doing what we should do more of, more of the time, with a
more alert sensitivity, and with greater skill.

Second, *TALK IT OUT!* has dominant tones of realism and prac-
ticality along with its clear message of encouraging all of us to deal
with conflict, earlier and with greater awareness. Particularly helpful in this connection is chapter 16, which not only details what his
4-step method can do, but warns about what no method can do.

The product of these two features, and others, is a kind of informed or intelligent enthusiasm for dealing with situations that
many of us, much of the time, prefer to avoid, postpone,
misinterpret, or that we just fail to recognize.

But enough of what will be obvious to readers of Dana's book, even early in their reading and in their reflecting on it. I join Dana in urging readers to act on that reading and reflecting.

Robert T. Golembiewski
Athens, Georgia
August 15, 1989

PREFACE

Interest in organizational conflict management has mush-roomed in recent years. We professionals in this emerging field, like specialists in other disciplines, talk to each other a lot. We write articles, publish scientific journals, hold conventions and produce books. These efforts have created an extensive body of knowledge available to mediators and academicians.

But I fear we have lost sight of whom we are serving.

Differences in attitudes, values, priorities, lifestyles, percep-tions and interests occur in every meaningful workplace relationship. These differences often give rise to conflicts that hurt our organizations and ourselves. But rarely are these conflicts brought to a mediator for resolution. Whether we are managers, staff, or technicians, we do the best we can on our own.

Where can the non-specialist turn for practical help in manag-ing day-to-day differences with others?

This book offers a simple tool to all of us who work with other people. The 4-Step Method is not intended for mediators, consult-ants or researchers, although it may provide insights to their work. This tool is designed especially for people who are not aspiring mediators, and who do not choose to bring their disputes to mediators for solution. It is for people who want more satisfaction and value from their workplace relationships. It is for people who desire an alternative to non-communication and power-play as ways of coping with interpersonal differences at work. It is for people who appreciate the value of building relationships, and who want to prevent differences from leading to destructive conflict. I think it may be for you.

Preview of . . .

THE 4-STEP METHOD

For Building Better Work Relationships

Step 1:   **FIND A TIME TO TALK**
Communication is necessary for managing all human differences.

Step 2:   **PLAN THE CONTEXT**
The right time, place, and setting will help your talk be successful.

Step 3:   **TALK IT OUT**
The **Opening**
>   Express appreciation
>   Express optimism
>   Reminders: The Cardinal Rules
>   State the issue

The **Invitation**

The **Dialogue**
>   Task #1: Stay engaged in the Essential Process
>   Task #2: Support Conciliatory Gestures

The **Breakthrough**

When these TASKS are performed during this special DIALOGUE in an appropriate CONTEXT, our attitudes can shift from "me-against-you" to "us-against-the-problem." This shift opens a window of opportunity for making a Deal that is good for both people and for their organization.

Step 4:   **MAKE A DEAL** (if needed)

Balanced

Behaviorally specific

Written

This practical consensus-building tool may be used by all members of organizations—not just managers or personnel specialists.

As mentioned previously, I fear that we mediators have lost sight of the obvious fact that most people who struggle toward better working relationships do it on their own, without professional assistance. The 4-Step Method has been carefully developed and tested so it can be used by non-professionals. The mediator's tool-kit has been emptied of all unessential, special-purpose, nice-to-know tools. Only the basics remain here, in this general-purpose tool for the non-specialist.

The intent of this book is to offer you a simple, effective method for managing differences in workplace relationships of importance. I will have failed in my mission if after reading it you say to yourself, "Okay, sounds good, but it's too complicated for me to use." Learning this Method alone will not make you an expert mediator or negotiator. But using it can empower you to build better relationships at work. I hope it will become part of your routine response to interpersonal differences. Best wishes!

A NOTE ON LANGUAGE

SPECIAL TERMS

A few key concepts are central to the message I intend to convey in this book, so it is important that I communicate them effectively. To do so, I will use words and phrases that have designated meanings. These are presented in the form of a special vocabulary that may differ from familiar definitions.

Terms that have special meanings will appear with the first letters capitalized to distinguish them from everyday speech. Each term will be defined when it first appears in the text. You will also find full definitions in the Glossary.

Special terms are listed here with the page number where each first appears:

The **4-Step Method,** page xvii

Other (the other person in your relationship), page 25

Wrong Reflexes, page 26

Non-communication (Wrong Reflex #1), page 28

Power-play (Wrong Reflex #2), page 28

Win-Lose Illusion, page 30

Boulder-in-the-Road Illusion, page 31

Bad-Person Illusion, page 34

Blips (Level 1 conflict), page 40

Clashes (Level 2 conflict), page 42

Crises (Level 3 conflict), page 43

Cardinal Rules, page 63

Dialogue (in Step 3 of the 4-Step Method), page 80

Breakthrough, page 84

TOWARD NON-SEXIST LANGUAGE

The evolution of the English language has left today's writers with a troublesome legacy—we have no common-gender singular personal pronouns.

The reader is no doubt familiar with popular attempts to solve this problem—generic masculine or feminine pronouns, combined terms ("he/she" and "her/him"), and pluralizing all pronouns ("they" and "them"). For various ethical and practical reasons, I reject these solutions.

My solution is to alternate masculine and feminine gender pronouns from paragraph to paragraph, or from situation to situation. By preparing the reader with this preliminary note, I hope to prevent diversion of your attention from the book's message that may be caused by alternating genders. I ask your indulgence for any remaining distraction you may experience.

PART 1

Chapter 1:

INTERPERSONAL TRAGEDIES:
The Human Cost of Conflict
at Work

Jon and Tara work together. Or, we should say they are *supposed* to work together. If their manager really knew how little work got done, she would have a fit. Their jobs require them to cooperate, but Jon finds cooperation impossible under the circumstances. It seems that every time he tries to get Tara to do her share of the work, she finds some new excuse. Jon winds up taking work home and spending extra hours doing what Tara is supposed to do. He's fed up. Last weekend Jon updated his resume and made some calls to friends in other companies. He decided he doesn't need to take this grief any longer.

Deana tries to remember what it was she liked about working here. Whatever attracted her to this company when she took the job has vanished. It's her supervisor, Kevin, who is the real problem. Her co-workers seem to ignore his rudeness, but she has too much pride to take it passively. Kevin just barks orders and never compliments her on jobs well done. Deana has thought about talking to him about how she feels, but wouldn't know what to say. He seems to be getting the idea that she doesn't like him, though. That worries her. She likes the job she does, and wouldn't want to leave, but working here is getting intolerable.

The Scope of the Problem

These are not soap opera scenarios. They are only two of the millions of real-life dramas played out daily in our workplaces. Organizations are teeming with interpersonal tragedies like these.

"Tragedy" is a strong word, but Jon and Deana are strongly affected. Workplace conflicts lead to stagnated careers, job stress, lowered productivity, lessened motivation—even termination and resignation. Three million involuntary job terminations and over 800,000 voluntary resignations occur each year in the United

States. How many of these departures broke a potentially productive bond between employee and employer?

For every terminated relationship, there are many more in which people maintain a tense and distant truce that brings them only meager satisfaction. Chronic, unresolved interpersonal conflicts cause needless stress and wastefully drain individual vitality and organizational resources. And, the United States represents only one-twentieth of the world's population. The magnitude of loss, in human and financial terms, is massive.

Tragedy Can Be Averted

So many of these tragedies are achingly unnecessary. There exists a way for colleagues in strained relationships to take charge of managing differences and resolving conflicts. They can regain trust and resume productive teamwork. The method is so simple it may seem simplistic. Yet it has the power to transform conflict into cooperation, mistrust into trust, and dysfunctional work teams into efficient partnerships. It harnesses natural constructive forces lying dormant within workplace relationships that can heal wounds caused by anger, insult, and hurt—the carnage of mutual revenge.

Differences, Needs, and Conflict

In every relationship, the differences that make us unique individuals are also sources of potential conflict between us. We differ in values, self-interests, priorities, and in many other ways. The greater the differences, the heavier the burden on our ability to manage those differences. The less effectively we manage differences, the more conflict we experience in the relationship.

Relationships satisfy needs. Every important relationship is a vehicle for bringing value to each partner. Our relationships with our peers, bosses, and subordinates hold potential for satisfying our needs to feel productive, to accomplish meaningful work, to produce widgets, and to earn paychecks. When our needs are met, we are satisfied, happy people—and productive workers.

Conflict drains the capacity of relationships to satisfy our needs. When we experience too much unresolved conflict, the relationship loses its ability to satisfy us. We are left alone, isolated, unable to do by ourselves what requires two to do.

Ironically, as we depend more heavily on a relationship to satisfy our needs, conflict is more likely to occur. High interdependency creates a climate in which conflict can grow more intense. Yet, to paraphrase poet John Donne, "No one is an island." Human nature and the nature of organizations require that we depend on others, that we be interdependent with others in satisfying our individual needs.

Figure 1:
How interdependency (strength of mutual need) between members is related to the likelihood of team conflict.

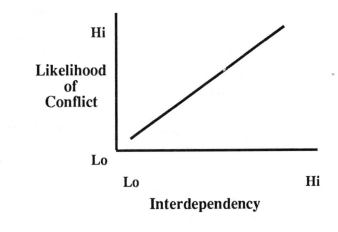

Room for Improvement

Interpersonal differences that breed the conflicts, and the tragedies, that each of us experiences from time to time can be better managed. No matter how skilled we are now, potential exists for us to be more satisfied and more productive. In this book a practical method for managing differences is introduced that eliminates the use of power plays and withdrawal—the typical yet counterproductive ways of coping with difficult situations. You can use the 4-Step Method to build better working relationships.

Chapter 2:

ORGANIZATIONAL TRAGEDIES: Measuring the Financial Cost of Conflict*

*   Adapted from "The Costs of Organizational Conflict" by Daniel Dana, *Organization Development Journal*, Fall 1984.

Unmanaged employee conflict is perhaps the largest reducible cost in organizations today—and probably the least recognized.

It is estimated that over 65% of performance problems result from strained relationships between employees—not from deficits in individual employees' skill or motivation.

Interdependent workplace relationships are a fertile soil from which conflict can sprout. Organizations are lush gardens hosting many flourishing varieties of this annoying and resource-sapping weed.

Now let's look at several ways this weed saps your organization's financial health and vitality.

Wasted Management Time

A classic management study* determined that 25% of the typical manager's time is spent responding to conflict. That figure rises to 30% for first line supervisors. Clearly, a fourth of the management salary budget represents no small investment in shielding productive work from the destructive effects of conflict.

Reduced Decision Quality

Decision-makers need valid information to render good decisions. Even when a good decision-making procedure is used, the best decision cannot be reached if information is withheld or distorted. If relationships between the decision-maker and information sources (co-workers, superiors, subordinates, support staff) are strained, the information received will probably be poor. Opinions

*   "A Survey of Managerial Interests with Respect to Conflict" by Kenneth W. Thomas and W. H. Schmidt, *Academy of Management Journal*, June 1966.

expressed during decision meetings may be based less on what is best for the company, and based more on what is in the private self-interest of the person providing the information.

When decision-making is a joint responsibility of two or more people whose relationship is conflicted, the problem is worsened. In this case, each individual is likely to regard the other's arguments as self-serving, or worse, intended to inflict harm. News media reports have suggested that the tragic decision to launch the ill-fated space shuttle *Challenger* in January 1986 was flawed by conflict among decision-makers.

The exact financial cost of a poor decision cannot be calculated since we can only speculate what might have happened had a different decision been made. Yet, given the often limitless range of alternatives, it is certain that decisions made under conditions of unmanaged conflict are seldom optimal.

Loss of Skilled Employees

When conflict appears irresolvable, management often sees dismissal or reassignment as the only option. The employee also may see only these options and resign. The result is the same. From a purely financial perspective the company has lost its investment in skills and job competencies—departing employees take their education and work experience with them.

Executives at Raytheon Corporation calculated the cost of replacing engineers. Reaching a figure that has been confirmed by other companies, they estimate that replacement cost is 1.5 times the total annual compensation package. This includes costs such as recruiting, interviewing, and retraining.

For example, an engineer who earns $40,000 costs the company about $60,000 when insurance, retirement funding, and other fringe benefits are included. Raytheon has determined that it costs $90,000 to replace departed employees.

Restructuring

Changes in the role positions of people in conflict can reduce the friction between them simply by reducing their required interaction. For example, altering one's job duties, changing the person to whom one reports, or changing the composition of work teams can reduce tensions between people. However, such restructuring incurs costs in at least two ways. First, work performed while people become oriented to new duties is generally less productive than work performed after one has settled into a situation.

The second cost is probably more damaging. Job roles should be designed to fit together so that the interrelated tasks of two or more employees are performed with maximum efficiency. Altering job design in order to accommodate a conflict between people will normally reduce efficiency in work flow.

Sabotage

Willful destruction of equipment, work processes, and reputations is probably the least easily recognized cost of conflict because most sabotage is hidden behind a cloak of "accidental" mistakes, "forgetfulness" or excuses of "being too busy." People who make mistakes or forget things aren't necessarily conscious of the causes of their errors, and can be quite sincere in explaining how the errors occurred. However, behavioral science has long known that so-called "errors" can often be due in part to unconscious hostility. A warehouse worker who "accidentally" leaves a $25,000 forklift running so that it rolls off a loading dock, or a manager who lets a confidential piece of information slip at a social gathering may be doing so partially because of angry feelings toward the company, a colleague, or some other target. Studies show that rejects of manufactured products, as well as "inventory shrinkage" from employee theft, decrease when relations are improved among workers and between employees and their supervisors.

Lowered Job Motivation

We work more effectively and efficiently when we are motivated to perform well. Enthusiasm and commitment are difficult to sustain when we experience chronic conflict with others at work. We may be busy at our desks for the required number of hours per day, yet our productivity will be less than optimal if our attention is on nagging tensions with a co-worker or boss.

Lost Work Time

Absenteeism can be caused by conflict in two ways: (1) lack of interest in work and a desire to avoid an unpleasant workplace, and (2) actual physical illness at least partially due to the emotional stress of chronic interpersonal conflict at work. Medical science has established that most physical illnesses are partly psychogenic. That is, our susceptibility to a virus or to breakdown of a physiological process in the body, and even proneness to injury, are increased when we are under stress produced by unrelieved interpersonal conflict at work.

Health Costs

Often, the physical illnesses that cause loss of work time also require medical attention, bringing the accompanying insurance claims. A company's insurance premium for employee health benefits is generally tied to the rate of claims. So the more health problems are caused by conflict, the greater the cost of insurance premiums.

There has been a dramatic increase in the number of stress-related worker's compensation claims in the last several years, due in part to the debilitating effects of stress.

Perhaps the most drastic health-related problem facing organizations today is employee alcoholism and other forms of substance abuse. Drugs have long been an appealing refuge from stress, including the stress of chronically strained relationships.

Estimating the Cost

Think of a specific workplace conflict that you have been involved in, or have observed. Using Figure 2 below, estimate the financial impact for each of the ways that the conflict may cost money. Then, add your estimates to get an indication of how much that particular conflict costs your organization.

Figure 2:
Estimating the cost of a specific workplace conflict.

COST FACTORS	YOUR ESTIMATE
Wasted management time	_____
Reduced decision quality	_____
Loss of employees	_____
Restructuring	_____
Sabotage	_____
Lowered job motivation	_____
Lost work time	_____
Health costs	_____
TOTAL COST:	_____

It's Up to You

Employees who know how to manage differences effectively are able to turn tense, unproductive relationships into harmonious, effective teams. Cost savings are significant. Productivity enhancement potential is substantial.

If you are a manager, enabling your employees to use the 4-Step Method may be the best decision you can make today.

Chapter 3:

DOES SELF-HELP HELP?
How This Book Might Save Your Project, Your Job, Your...

Often, while reading self-help books, I think to myself, "It sounds good, but I doubt I will remember much of this a month from now." I am skeptical of suggestions that a quick dose of advice will have long-term impact in real-life situations.

The Problem of Self-Control

Much of the advice in self-help books urges us to alter our perceptions, thoughts, beliefs, motives, intentions, attitudes, or values. Once these changes are accomplished, it is suggested, then some personal problem related to the subject of the book will be solved. Perhaps so.

My skepticism lies in the difficulty of accomplishing these changes. Perceptions, thoughts, attitudes, and the like are invisible "mental events" that occur privately within our heads. They are not observable by others. Mental events are extremely difficult to control or manipulate. Uncomfortable feelings, unwanted thoughts, disturbing perceptions, and self-destructive motives can intrude, despite our efforts at self-control. For most of us, our willpower is seldom adequate to fend off the challenge of strong, persistent thoughts and feelings.

Behavior is easier to control than mental activity. Behavioral events are observable and can be controlled by the behaver. Behavior can be described in concrete terms, like a physical object can be described. We can say, "I'm going to write that report, even though I don't want to." The writing is behavior; the wanting to is a mental event. Behavior can be seen or heard. Precisely defined behavior either is or isn't; it happens or doesn't happen. We may dispute the motives that give rise to the behavior, but the fact of its occurrence is indisputable.

An Illustration

The United States' government has been attempting for decades to remove racism from American workplaces. Some critics have faulted the effort on the grounds that it is impossible to "legislate morality." In other words, they argue that some employees will hold prejudicial attitudes toward people of other races regardless of laws to the contrary. In truth, racism is a category of mental events happening in people's heads that cannot be directly affected by commandments that it not exist. Many of us who grew up learning racist attitudes now strive to eradicate traces of these unwanted ideas. We struggle against the effect of decades of socialization.

With Equal Employment Opportunity (EEO) legislation, the United States Congress has made it illegal for companies to consider race or ethnicity in the selection of employees. EEO makes no pretense of altering our attitudes toward members of other races. It simply requires that certain of the barriers that have prevented minorities from entering the workforce in the past be removed. As a result, workplaces are now more racially integrated than before EEO was implemented.

We know for a fact that, when people of different races have more contact with each other, attitudes change. Working together tests the validity of our racial stereotypes, and, naturally, they diminish. So, EEO legislation is directed at a change in behavior, not in personal beliefs or values. However, by controlling hiring decisions (behavioral events), the government is *indirectly* affecting racism (mental events) in organizational life.

Behavioral Prescription

This book offers no prescriptions about how you should think or feel in interpersonal conflict. As an adult, your mental events have been largely fixed through decades of life experience. Admittedly, our patterns of thinking and feeling can be changed, but probably not by simply reading this or any other self-help book. That is the task of psychotherapy and other more intensive paths to personal change.

The 4-Step Method is a *behavioral* prescription, a recipe consisting of behavioral ingredients. When its directions are followed, the recipe can indirectly change how you and your Other* feel (reduced anger, increased trust), what attitudes you have (increased optimism about your relationship and about your ability to cooperate), and your intentions toward each other (less hostile, more friendly).

Link Between Behavior and Attitude

The link between EEO's behavioral ingredients and the resulting changes in racial attitudes may not be obvious. Just how and why does a behavioral event change a mental event in a predictable way? That is where behavioral science enters the picture. Contrary to critics' claims that EEO legislation does not reduce underlying racism, scientific research has demonstrated that working with others of different races does in fact change our attitudes and reduce our negative racial stereotypes.

The link between this 4-Step recipe's behavioral ingredients and the resulting interpersonal harmony may not be obvious either. Just how and why does communicating as the Method recommends

---

*   The term "Other" with a capital "O" will be used in this book when referring to the other person in our two-person, ongoing, interdependent relationships.

result in reduced conflict, increased trust, and better teamwork? Part 4 of this book is dedicated to explaining this link.

But the 4-Step Method is not simply untested theory, to be taken on faith. Its effectiveness has been demonstrated consistently. It works even if you are skeptical, and it works even if you don't understand why. It is only necessary that you make the deliberate choice to use the Method as it is designed to be used.

Figure 3:
Two ways of trying to change mental events.

1) **Attitude prescription (the direct approach)**

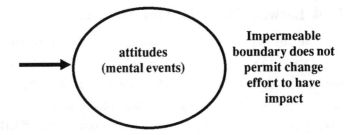

2) **Behavioral prescription (the indirect approach)**

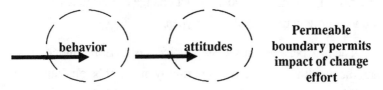

How *This* Self-Help Book Can Help

So, this book's central purpose is not to give the reader self-insight or to label communication styles. Rather, it offers you very practical, concrete, behaviorally specific advice for managing differences that can erupt in destructive conflict and erode the value of your important workplace relationships.

Wherever you are as you read these words, you live and work with other people. I invite you to test the 4-Step Method for yourself. Use it just once in a work relationship that matters to you. Then watch the results. Notice how trust is renewed and cooperative spirit is resumed. Then continue to use this simple communication tool to get more satisfaction from working with Others.

Chapter 4:

WHY DO WE SELF-DESTRUCT?

In win-lose conflicts at work, I hurt myself as much as I hurt my Other. Why do I find it so difficult to approach my Other in a both-gain* spirit?

A few key obstacles impair our ability to manage differences in ongoing interdependent relationships at work. These obstacles fall into two categories: "Wrong Reflexes" and "Illusions." Together, they account for much of our puzzling human tendency to behave self-destructively, to persist in win-lose struggles that damage our own self-interests. We seem to be unable to learn a better way, in spite of a multitude of prior episodes in any lifetime that can only be termed failures to manage differences well.

Figure 4:
Illusions (perceptions and beliefs) lead to Wrong Reflexes (behaviors), which lead to self-destructive outcomes.

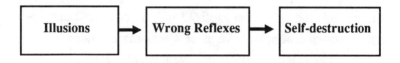

---

*   The expression "both-gain" is used rather than the more common term "win-win" to avoid the inherently competitive definition of winning. By implication, if there is a winner, there must also be a loser. The intent of this book is to suggest that both participants can gain—without losing and without defeating the Other.

WRONG REFLEXES

The Way We Were

Our evolutionary legacy haunts us. In simpler times, before humans lived in communities larger than a few dozen, when organizations as workplaces had not yet been invented, and before humanistic values had developed, our reflexes served us well. In those times, it was useful to assume:

1) that the best way to avoid danger was to escape, to remove ourselves from the presence of the threat, and

2) that, if escape were blocked, the best way to protect ourselves from a threat was to meet force with force in the hope of defeating the Other.

This pair of automatic assumptions is popularly known as the "flight or fight" instinct.

These reflexes were very adaptive for our pre-historic ancestors. The extent to which they were functioning determined how successfully the individual survived and passed genetic characteristics on to descendants. In other words, these automatic responses in dangerous situations eventually became instinctive, part of our biological nature. Today, we are the descendants of those who survived the dangers. We are the result of natural selection pressures that favored individuals who had what are, in modern life, "Wrong Reflexes."

Times Have Changed

Why are these reflexes wrong today when they were right in the past? Much has changed. Today, the dangers posed to us in the organizational jungle are seldom physical threats. Escape (flight) is a costly option, since we are in long-term interdependent relationships—we have to go to our jobs tomorrow and work with the same people. Resolving a conflict by terminating these relationships is a drastic measure.

The alternative reflex, using force to defeat the opponent (fight), is no better. Physical assault is not acceptable in our culture as a means of dealing with people who differ from us. Threats, intimidation, and coercive power to win our way may succeed in the short run. But such tactics lay the groundwork for future retaliation by the other person. Using force is a poor method of handling differences in ongoing interdependent relationships—those that matter most.

But our bodies don't know that anything has changed since we lived in caves. Our genetic code, including the genes that control these behavioral mechanisms, is nearly identical to the Neanderthals. Our reflexes—the ones we inherited from our survivor ancestors—still prompt us to act as if we are confronting a tiger on the plains of the ancient continent of Pangaea. We still unconsciously assume that each confrontation is a win-lose encounter, where only one of us can win and the other must lose. We still reflexively respond to threats by trying to withdraw or escape from interaction. When trapped and escape is blocked, we still draw upon our resources to coerce the other into submission or compliance. This reaction is not conscious, and it is universal. Every normal human being responds this way.

Modern Forms

Of course, we no longer fight with spears and flee into the forest. We use updated forms of the ancient impulses. Physical attack has been replaced by tactics like cutting off funds, overriding objections, and stating ultimatums. Physical flight has been replaced by avoiding meetings, failing to return phone calls, and not speaking up when we object to another's actions.

Now that we have evolved the vehicle of language to express ourselves, we have developed a curious hybrid of fight and flight, "passive aggression." Favorite forms of passive aggression include making uncomplimentary remarks to associates about the Other, quietly undermining support of her projects, and finding excuses for not responding to a request. Having language enables us to inflict harm on the Other while concealing our aggressive motives.

Disguised in modern forms, our ancient impulses are still very much with us. These Wrong Reflexes are the two and only two means of coping with conflict that our instinct-driven bodies allow us to recognize:

1) **Non-communication** ("flight"), an effort to withdraw from the relationship

2) **Power-play** ("fight"), an effort to defeat the Other

ILLUSIONS

Illusions are distorted perceptions that do not convey accurate information about the "external world," as philosophers refer to everything outside our skin. Our behavior is based on the assumption that our perceptions are accurate. A person who believes that he is an alien from Jupiter who is being persecuted by the CIA is behaving reasonably and appropriately—assuming it is true that he is actually an alien from Jupiter and is being persecuted by the CIA. Perception is the process of interpreting the external world so that we may act in it.

Whose Truth Is True?

Perceptions are illusions when they are judged by someone else to be inaccurate interpretations of reality. When the someone else is the surrounding society, we often call the problem "mental illness." When the someone else is our co-worker, we call the problem "conflict." Most of us accept majority-rule as a way of deciding what is, in truth, external reality. That is, if most people say something is true, then it must be true. However, this way of deciding about reality is imperfect. The majority of Europeans believed the world was flat until fifteenth-century explorers discovered that we can go to the East by sailing West.

In typical interpersonal conflicts on the job, there are only two versions of the truth—yours and mine. It is often quite unclear whose version is more correct. Appeals for support by majority-rule ("everyone agrees with me, just ask around") seldom succeed in convincing the Other to accept the correctness of our position. Persistence in the conflict not only achieves our goal of inflicting harm on the Other—it also undermines our own interests. To the degree that we harm our own interests, we self-destruct.

Illusions are universal—that is, they occur in everyone. Therefore, we cannot claim that they result from the Other's psychological problems. They are normal, an integral part of our biological perceptual mechanisms—we are simply built that way.

Three illusions shed especially revealing light on how we self-destruct in interpersonal conflict:

> The "Win-Lose Illusion"
>
> The "Bad-Person Illusion"
>
> The "Boulder-in-the-Road Illusion"

The Win-Lose Illusion

Our needs are fundamentally incompatible; only one of us can prevail.

Some authors urge us to appreciate that conflict provides a valuable opportunity for creative problem-solving, synergy, and personal growth. My chosen career is conflict resolution, and I am regarded by some as an expert in the field. In a fit of self-disclosure, I hereby report to you that I personally have great difficulty, when engaged in conflict, appreciating these virtues. I initially react to most conflicts as if they are win-lose situations. My Other and I argue different positions on an issue, and I assume that the incompatibility of our demands means that the outcome must necessarily favor one of us over the other. Pending calmer reflection, I feel that only one of us can be right, only one of us can get what we want—the other must lose. Only with great effort can I imagine the possibility that neither of us must lose, that a both-gain outcome is worth seeking. Until then, the possibility of a both-gain outcome does not enter my view of the realm of possibilities. The illusion is that a win-lose outcome is inevitable when, in fact, both-gain alternatives often exist.

I don't believe I am unique in this odd blindness. Nor do I believe that transcending the Win-Lose Illusion is easy. Nor, I'm afraid, is clear vision of both-gain possibilities within the reach of the vast majority of us. I believe it is a futile exercise to propose that we educate the population of the globe to recognize the possibility of both-gain outcomes to our interpersonal conflicts.

But all is not gloom. It may be true that the Win-Lose Illusion will regularly blind us as we struggle to manage differences with others day-to-day. Happily, however, success in using the 4-Step

Method does not require that either you or your Other is able to avoid this troublesome trickster of perception.

The Bad-Person Illusion

Our conflict is the direct result of your incompetence, cruelty, stupidity, or other defect; it can only be resolved if you recognize and correct your defects.

When differences have been managed poorly, that is, by means of the Wrong Reflexes, certain attitudes about our Other become entrenched over time and seem absolutely correct. We grow to think that he is bad in some way—mean, corrupt, immoral, malicious, evil. In more generous moments, we may offer the concession that the Other's behavior is due to being simply crazy or disturbed, suggesting that she is not fully in control of her behavior.

By believing that the conflict is a direct consequence of our Other's personal defects, we are able to absolve ourselves of responsibility for contributing to the problem. We comfort ourselves with the belief that the other person is at fault, and that we are innocent, hapless victims.

A Two-Way Street

But notice a curious fact about the Bad-Person Illusion: It is almost always reciprocal. That is, each participant believes the other is at fault due to an assortment of personal defects. The regularity of the Bad-Person Illusion being a two-way street suggests that it may not be true that one of the persons is in fact evil or crazy. To believe that the cause of our conflict lies in inherently bad personal characteristics of the Other is a distortion of reality. The cause is differentness, not badness.

Even if we insist that the Other is bad, our value judgment does not lead toward resolution. Since he probably feels quite the reverse, and holds us in low esteem as we do him, he is not about to accept our judgment and acquiesce to our values. Negotiations based on mutual Bad-Person judgements only lead to impasse.

In long term conflict, our hostile, hurtful, and even self-destructive behavior may seem to make the Bad-Person belief come true. That is, under the stress of the moment, we can act crazy, and do bad things. In this way, the illusion becomes a self-fulfilling prophesy.

But even when we behave cruelly or senselessly, we justify our own "bad" behavior as resulting from having been mercilessly provoked by the Other. We insist that it is atypical of us to act that way, whereas the bad behavior exhibited by the Other reveals deep flaws in his personality. We find it difficult to regard the Other's behavior in that same, understanding light.

The Bad-Person Illusion, then, is the distorted image that the Other's behavior derives from his evil or crazy nature. His behavior is not interpreted, as is more often the case, as a natural, normal response to the conflict between us. Even when there is some majority-rule support that our version of reality is correct, such as a psychiatrist's diagnosis, the illusion still plays a role. It causes us to exaggerate the difference between us and our Other in terms of how justifiable and situation-dependent the "bad" behaviors are. That is, we excuse ourselves but are unable to excuse our Other.

An Illustration

In the 1980's, the Ayatolla Khomeini of Iran seemed to many Americans to be a bad person. Allegedly, he sponsored terrorism and hostage-taking, placed explosive mines in the Persian Gulf in violation of international shipping law, and killed and tortured his own citizens who did not conform to his beliefs. We would agree, would we not, that the Ayatolla was either evil or crazy or both?

Curiously, the Ayatolla referred to the United States as the "Great Satan," the source of evil in the world. Americans, who believe in democracy, and human rights, and due process under the law—evil? How can this be?

Although it strains my mediator's neutrality to do so, I suspect that the Ayatolla behaved reasonably and appropriately within the context of his system of values and perception of the world. I suspect that he was capable of compassion and concern for others. He was not, I suspect, "insane."

The Iran-US conflict of the 1980's, then, featured a reciprocal illusion that the other is, by its nature, evil—the Bad-Person Illusion on an international scale.

Designed to achieve interpersonal, not international, peace, the 4-Step Method surely is inadequate for resolving the Iran-US conflict. Still, it does seem that a foreign policy of Non-communication with Iran and other Others around the globe precludes any possibility of resolution, just as the Wrong Reflex of withdrawal from relationship has that same effect on prospects for collaborative teamwork with our Others on the job.

Is the Bad-Person Illusion a fatal flaw of human nature that makes it impossible to manage our differences constructively? Fortunately, using the 4-Step Method does not require that we or our Others must free ourselves from this most human perceptual trap.

The Boulder-in-the-Road Illusion

Our differences are irreconcilable; agreement is impossible.

When we encounter a difference with our boss, colleague, or employee, and when agreement or cooperation is required to proceed further, an especially unfortunate misperception arises. It often seems that differences between us are so huge—his character is so devoid of virtue, she is so crazy, our values are so opposite—that reconciliation is impossible. A "boulder in the road" totally blocks further progress. Faced with the hopelessness of this impasse, we may feel forced to choose between the two Wrong Reflexes—either minimize or withdraw entirely from interaction (Non-communication), or muster our resources to crush the resistance put up by the Other (Power-play). Tragically, limiting ourselves to these two ineffective options can lead to escalated hostilities and even stalled careers, job termination, or pointless legal entanglement.

Why do we perceptually exaggerate the difficulty, to the point of impossibility, of reconciling our differences? Why do we see no way around the boulder in the road? It sometimes seems that the only thing that can be agreed upon is that agreement is impossible.

In fact, there nearly always is a way around the boulder. Rarely are the underlying self-interests of each participant exactly opposite on any issue of genuine importance. Even when self-interests are incompatible, the search for reasonable compromise can find a better path for each participant than continued conflict.

THE CHALLENGE TO GOOD TEAMWORK

We are, at times, victims of our own instincts. We labor under illusions that one must win and one must lose, that the problem would be solved if only our stubborn Other would admit fault, and, failing these unlikely outcomes, our differences are irreconcilable.

To cope with this awful state of affairs, we see our only options as Non-communication to keep things smooth, or, when interaction is required, Power-play as a desperate effort to win or at least avoid losing.

There is an alternative. It is remarkably simple and effective, even though our instinctive blinders often prevent us from seeing it. Using it can produce a surprising transformation that allows recon- ciliation of differences without withdrawing, without overpowering, and without losing. There is a way around the boulder in the road. The 4-Step Method helps you and your Other find another route.

An Attitude Shift: Breakthrough

In the search for solutions, our initial challenge is to accept the possibility that a both-gain solution exists. We need to achieve a climate where both participants can express a shared interest in resolving the problem in a fair, if yet undiscovered, way. We need a shift in attitudes from "you-against-me" to "us-against-the-prob- lem." In this more trusting climate, fair compromise and mutual concessions can be more safely discussed. Such an attitude shift would truly be a breakthrough.

How can this Breakthrough be achieved? The structure and con- text of the 4-Step Method prevent the Wrong Reflexes from occurring. The attitude shift does not result from persuasion or reasoning, but from psychological forces toward harmony (to be dis- cussed in Chapter 20) that are harnessed by the special dialogue occurring in Step 3.

Once this attitude shift occurs, a solution can be found. If a both-gain solution is possible, it can be mutually sought. If a both-gain outcome is not possible, we can more safely make reasonable compromises in the more trusting climate that the 4-Step Method produces. In either case, a way has been found around the boulder in the road that does not demand a sacrificial loser.

Chapter 5:

THE THREE LEVELS OF CONFLICT

Some conflicts are hardly noticeable as they ebb and flow through our daily social encounters. Others grow into intense disputes that spawn interpersonal tragedies. The severity of conflict ranges from insignificant *Blips* through a middle range of *Clashes* to severe *Crises* that threaten the survival of the relationship.

Just as a golfer selects the proper club for the shot, and a mechanic chooses the right tool for the job, different levels of conflict call for different strategies. The 4-Step Method is designed for conflicts that are more troublesome than passing minor annoyances, but that have not reached crisis proportions. This chapter will describe the level of conflict that the Method is designed to resolve—Level 2 Clashes. It will also offer suggestions for dealing constructively with Blips and Crises.

Figure 5:
Blips, Clashes, and Crises—the three levels of conflict.

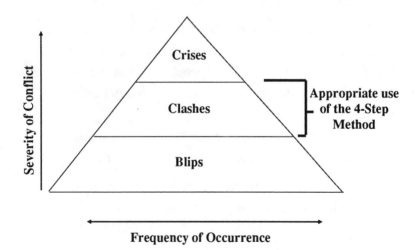

LEVEL 1: BLIPS

Worklife without Blips would be boring. Even if this were not so, Blips are inevitable. It is hardly imaginable that a single day spent with people could be free of minor annoyances. But these Blips pose no threat to the relationship, nor do they produce disharmony that breaks down teamwork and blocks satisfaction of needs.

Example

A co-worker uses your coffee cup to water plants in the office. You have asked her to find another water vessel, but she still uses your cup occasionally when you are not there. If you are otherwise cordial and cooperative, this annoyance can probably be handled by additional assertions of your wishes. A special meeting as called for by the 4-Step Method is probably unnecessary.

Still, Blips can grow more severe if poorly handled over time. How can we prevent the needless escalation of Level 1 Blips into Level 2 Clashes or Level 3 Crises?

The simplest advice is to refrain from resorting to those outdated Wrong Reflexes—Non-communication and Power-play. These behaviors antagonize other people, and they prevent the communication that is necessary to limit misunderstandings. In other words:

1) Do not walk out, hang up, or otherwise use termination of contact as a retaliatory tactic.

2) Do not use threats, intimidation, or force to pressure your Other to comply with your wishes.

The Gift Exchange

As Blips accumulate and tension mounts, communication breaks down. Before Level 1 Blips become Level 2 Clashes, you can use an intriguing behavioral device to trigger a release of tension in your relationship.

The device consists of initiating an unexpected "gift"—a conciliatory gesture—to the other person. Invite your co- worker to lunch or stop by his office to ask about his children. Compliment your boss on her recent award, or offer to get your subordinate a cup of coffee. An automatic psychological reflex causes friendly gestures like these to spark a reciprocal gesture—a "gift exchange." If a genuine gift exchange happens, tension can quickly subside and trust may be renewed.

The reflex that prompts your Other to reciprocate your gift is present in everyone. However, certain personality factors can block it from occurring in some people. So, you cannot be sure it will work every time you try it. But your gift costs little, and it can trigger a valuable shift in your relationship from distance to closeness. You accept the risk that your gift will be rejected, that you might be seen as giving in, or as setting a precedent that you do not want to be bound to in the future. Taking this risk requires courage. Paradoxically, allowing ourselves to appear weak by our vulnerability to rejection requires strength.

What happens if your Other does not return your gift? If your initiatives do not trigger a response after two or three attempts, then it probably will not do so in the future.

A note of caution: The dynamics of the gift-exchange are psychological and emotional, not rational and logical. The impulse to reciprocate is an unconscious response. In business negotiations, bargaining strategies are often quite rational. The gift-exchange may not work because skilled negotiators are often trained to divert psychological inducements to make concessions. Although the gift-exchange can be effectively used in business negotiations, be especially careful not to initiate a gift that weakens your bargaining position.

LEVEL 2: CLASHES

The 4-Step Method, the central message of this book, is designed to help us manage differences in good relationships. Clashes happen in good relationships.

Despite our best efforts, Blips sometimes accumulate and grow into Clashes. How do we know when the line has been crossed? Indications are:

- Repeated arguments about the same issue, perhaps spread over days or weeks.
- Arguing over an increasing number of issues.
- Feeling less cooperative toward the Other.
- Feeling less trusting of the Other's honest goodwill toward us.
- Remaining angry at the Other for a longer period, perhaps hours or days.
- Beginning to privately question the value of the relationship.

Example

Your colleague on a project team has made a number of mistakes that you have worked overtime to correct. When confronted, he shrugs it off, saying that you are being too picky. Your resentment grows as you are unable to get him to respond to your complaint.

Part 2 of this book will describe in detail how to use the 4- Step Method to produce solutions to the issues on which you and your Other clash.

LEVEL 3: CRISES

Most of us, at points in life, encounter differences so deep that even regular communication as the 4-Step Method suggests will not produce satisfaction. Crises call for more help than this self-help procedure can provide. How can we distinguish Crises from Clashes? Indications are:

- You have irreversibly decided to terminate the relationship.

- You fear that your Other will act unilaterally to terminate the relationship.

- You sense that the relationship is psychologically unhealthy, and fear that you are vulnerable to emotional harm by remaining in it.

- Either you or the Other is so emotionally upset and volatile that there is a risk of physical violence.

Example

Your boss rated you "unsatisfactory" in your latest performance appraisal. Believing that the evaluation is unfair, you have attempted to speak with your boss, only to be told that it is a closed case. Your resentment about not being given an opportunity to rebut the negative appraisal is eroding your loyalty to the company.

Option: Request assistance from a qualified personnel representative or ombudsman who can mediate the dispute.

What can you do about severe conflicts? In the most pessimistic analysis, intentionally using the Wrong Reflexes as a coping strategy is an option that is still available to you:

Non-communication. You may choose to maintain enough emotional distance from the Other to protect you from harm.

Power-play. You may choose to use threat and manipulation to avoid losing what may be a continuous win-lose conflict.

Of course, neither of these options can bring you satisfaction in the relationship or will serve the interests of your employer, and with time are likely to lead to further deterioration. Before resigning yourself to such an unhappy fate, consider more constructive solutions:

- Use a mediator (see Chapter 14: "Mediation"), and/or

- Use a counselor or your employee assistance program to gain emotional support and explore how you can best deal with the difficult situation you face.

Crises are dangerous. You may face a painful choice of terminating the relationship or staying in a situation that holds no prospect of satisfactory solution. Please read Chapter 17 ("When It Works, When It Won't") before deciding to use the 4-Step Method.

Chapter 6:

MANAGING CULTURAL DIFFERENCES:
A Growing Challenge to Organizations

Karen likes to spend a half-hour each week privately with each of her employees to sound out their concerns about the office. David, her colleague in another work unit, thinks this practice is not only a waste of time, but also is unwise. "Why take the lid off Pandora's box?" he asks.

Guillermo, 32 years old and married with four children, recently declined a promotion that would require moving to a city 800 miles away. He explained that he does not want to leave his seven brothers and sisters and their families who live nearby. Luther, who works closely with Guillermo, thinks it is a sign of immaturity that his Hispanic colleague would give up this career opportunity for reasons that he should have grown out of by this age. Luther's respect for Guillermo is reduced one notch.

James, who grew up in an inner-city black neighborhood, is being interviewed for a sales position by Lisa, who is white. Lisa notices that James does not maintain eye contact while listening to her. Lisa forms an immediate impression that James lacks assertiveness, and will probably not be able to handle important clients.

Some Facts

Consider these startling statistics:

Figure 6:
Non-white share of labor force.*

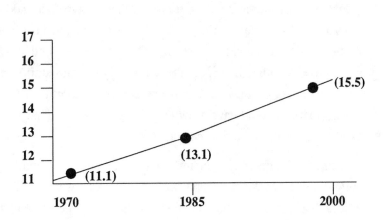

Figure 7:
Share of labor force, by gender.*

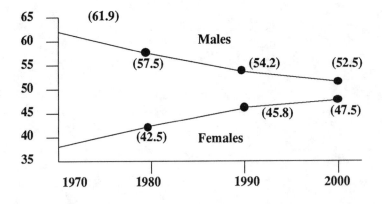

By the year 2000, only 15% of the new additions to the workforce between 1985 and 2000 will be native, white males.*

The future is inevitable: American organizations are increasingly multi-cultural. The writing is on the wall: The challenge of managing culture-based differences at work is upon us.

In anticipation of this challenge, "managing cultural diversity" has become one of the hottest topics in the training industry. No fewer than 40 presentations at the 1989 national conference of the American Society for Training and Development addressed cross-cultural issues. Several consulting firms specialize in training that is targeted at helping organizations manage cultural diversity.

Facing the Challenge

A common response to this challenge is to raise the awareness of dominant-culture employees about the values and norms of members of other groups. David seems unaware that women tend to focus on relationship issues more than do men. Luther seems unaware that Hispanics place a higher value on extended family relationships than do most Anglos. Lisa seems unaware that blacks from some sub-cultures keep eye contact while speaking but not while listening, the reverse of the pattern typical of many whites.

Information like this is typically conveyed in cross-cultural training programs for dominant-culture employees. The assumption underlying such "awareness" training is that, after completion of the program, participants are supposed not only to recognize dif-

*   Source: *Workforce 2000: Work and Workers for the Twenty-first Century*. Indianapolis: Hudson Institute, 1987.

ferences, but also to change how they behave toward minority-culture people.

But, to achieve maximum benefit, information should be supplemented with behaviorally specific skills, or "tools," that give trainees actual techniques for solving a problem. Awareness is a first step, but alone is insufficient.

Reasons for Concern

Simply informing members of today's organizations about cultural differences is an incomplete approach to helping workmates bridge the gaps that impair cooperative work. Consider these factors:

1) RESISTANCE TO CHANGE. Majority-culture trainees may perceive that some personal shortcoming is being "fixed" by the training. Or, they may feel personally blamed for creating the inequities often encountered by minority-culture employees. Or, they may perceive, perhaps accurately, that the political power they enjoy as dominant-culture members is in jeopardy of being eroded by cross-cultural training. In short, they perceive that their self-interests are threatened.

When self-interest is threatened, defensiveness is automatically and instinctively aroused. When we feel defensive, we naturally and inevitably resist. Resistance can take many forms. Resistance to cross-cultural training can take forms such as

- refusing to allow insight into one's own behavior patterns to occur, or

- doubting the validity of the information, or

- criticizing the usefulness of the training, or

- perceiving the seminar leader, especially if he is of another culture, as being self-serving or prejudiced against the dominant culture, or

- simply forgetting or not using the information

In any case, resistance can undermine awareness-building efforts to bridge culture-based differences in the organization. To be sure, cross-cultural training can be a powerful and enlightening experience for those who seek to participate. It may not be so for those on whom it is thrust.

2) INHERENT BIAS. By providing training primarily for the "benefit" of dominant-culture members, cultural diversity programs place the onus of responsibility on members of the dominant culture to accommodate to the needs of other groups. The program design may implicitly assume that minority-culture members already know plenty about the dominant culture's norms and values. Or, seminar designers may feel that members of minority groups do not have as much responsibility for bridging cultural differences because they are the "low-power" party in the cross-cultural relationship.

This bias may or may not be intended. Even when intended, it may not be explicitly stated by the seminar leader. But if dominant-culture members are discriminately selected for training, or if training is directed at the "culture-blindness" of the dominant group, it is a message heard clearly by trainees.

Further, organizations that focus cross-cultural training on the awareness-deficiencies of dominant-culture people do a disservice to their minority and female employees—doing so perpetuates dominant-culture dominance. How? By being given primary responsibility for change, dominant-culture people are still in the driver's seat, they are still in power, they are still the ones with options. Minorities are kept dependent on the choices of dominant-culture members—if a white male trainee chooses to do nothing differently after training, then discrimination continues. So, cross-cultural training may backfire. It may maintain the very power imbalance that it seeks to alter.

3) NO TOOLS. In spite of these factors, let's grant that information about cultural differences is presented, and that it is learned. Awareness is achieved. Then what? What is the program participant asked to DO with it? What practical behavioral tools are provided that will enable him to manage differences with minority colleagues more effectively? Too often, trainees are left in the dilemma of the automobile mechanic who knows how to fix the problem, but lacks the tools to apply her knowledge.

An Alternative

So, what alternatives exist to training that is based only on building cultural awareness? How can we achieve a more integrated multi-cultural workforce, in which differences arising from cultural values and behavioral norms are not only recognized, but are also effectively managed?

While information about cultural values and norms is a useful basis for change, an effective program must include behavioral tools—tools with which BOTH majority- and minority-culture members can initiate problem-solving dialogue. Tools that are equally powerful, no matter whose hands are at the controls. Tools that make no value judgment, explicitly or implicitly, about whose side of a difference is more right. Tools that work.

The 4-Step Method is such a tool. It enables an individual of any ethnicity and of either sex to initiate dialogue in search of common ground with Others. Our cultural backgrounds are one source of differences, an important one. But differences that impair workplace productivity arise from many sources. As individuals, we are more than just our cultural identity. The 4-Step Method is a tool for managing differences regardless of their origin—cross-cultural or "cross-personal."

Whether you are Asian, Hispanic, black, or white, female or male, you can empower yourself to implement your own private "cultural diversity program." Use the 4-Step Method to engage colleagues with whom you clash in dialogue to seek mutually acceptable solutions to workplace problems. Your differences on the disputed issues may arise from culture-based values and styles of behavior, and it is certainly useful to learn how your Other differs from you in these ways. But, underneath our culture and our gender, we share fundamentally human qualities. The 4-Step Method draws on our basic human characteristics to bring us to common ground.

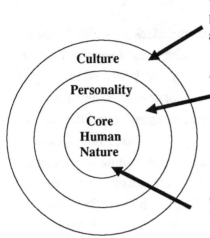

Figure 8:
The effectiveness of the 4-Step Method is influenced by culture, personality, and core human nature.

Values and norms that are shared by all or most individuals within a culture (learned)

Attitudes, beliefs, temperament, and behavioral style of individuals within one's own culture (learned, and/or influenced by heredity)

Psychological and behavioral characteristics that are common to all people, regardless of culture (inherited)

Culture-compatibility

To be sure, certain parts of the Method are more compatible with the norms of some cultures than with others. But choosing to avoid the Wrong Reflexes, and taking initiative to solve an interpersonal problem, are unfamiliar and challenging behaviors for most of us, no matter which culture we call home. Our tendencies to Noncommunicate and to use Power-plays, and the Illusions from which these reflexive behaviors spring, are rooted in universal human nature. So, our reluctance to use the 4-Step Method is as much personal as it is cultural.

In fact, this Method presents an opportunity for women and members of non-dominant ethnic groups who find themselves disempowered by the prevailing politics of their organizations to take charge of managing differences in relationships that matter. Large-scale social change may be coming, but why wait? Act now to improve the relationships that affect you today.

Still, we have much to learn about the impact of various cultures on the effectiveness of the 4-Step Method. Please report your experiences to Mediation Training Institute International, Attn: Cross-cultural Research, P.O. Box 6261, Wolcott, Connecticut 06716 USA.

PART 2

Chapter 7:

A skeleton view of THE 4-STEP METHOD For Building Better Work Relationships

The next several chapters will examine in detail each step of the 4-Step Method. Before diving into the trees, an overview of the forest may provide a useful perspective.

Step 1:   **FIND A TIME TO TALK**
            Communication is necessary for managing all human
            differences.

Step 2:   **PLAN THE CONTEXT**
            The right time, place, and setting will help your talk be
            successful.

Step 3:   **TALK IT OUT**
            The **Opening**

                    Express appreciation

                    Express optimism

                    Reminders: The Cardinal Rules

                    State the issue

            The **Invitation**

            The **Dialogue**

                    Task #1: Stay engaged in the Essential Process

                    Task #2: Support Conciliatory Gestures

            The **Breakthrough**

Step 4:   **MAKE A DEAL** (if needed)
            Balanced
            Behaviorally specific
            Written

Chapter 8:

THE CARDINAL RULES

At the core of the 4-Step Method are the Cardinal Rules, outlawing the Wrong Reflexes. The effectiveness of this path to two-person productivity flows directly from the prohibition of those two self-destructive impulses. The Cardinal Rules are the interpersonal equivalent of naval "rules of engagement" that assert one's rights while preventing escalation of hostilities.

#1: *Do Not Withdraw* from communication, whether from frustration and hopelessness, or as a retaliatory tactic directed against the Other.

#2: *Do Not Use Power-Plays* to "win" a power struggle by defeating the Other via threats, ultimatums, coercion, or physical force.

Using these Cardinal Rules as your personal rules of engagement, in the 4-Step Method and in routine workplace interactions, helps to manage differences and maintain productive and satisfying relationships.

Chapter 9:

Step 1
FIND A TIME TO TALK

Recall that one of our Wrong Reflexes is Non-communication. We too eagerly disengage from the Other, withdraw, escape to safety behind a wall of inaccessibility.

Being unavailable for contact ensures that conflict remains unresolved. A sage once said, "Abstinence from communication is the essence of conflict." Without doubt, no resolution is possible without communication. So, the first and most fundamental requirement is to establish a time in which communication can occur.

You are fortunate if your Other has read this book and is familiar with the 4-Step Method. It works even better when both people know it. But on many occasions you alone will initiate and actively manage the process. So we will assume that you are solely responsible.

Selling

It is likely that your Other will be reluctant to talk with you about your differences. Her Wrong Reflex to avoid "unpleasant encounters" may be strong. So, you may need to sell her on the idea of joining you in a Dialogue that is explicitly focused on the issues that divide you.

How can you sell it? Let's draw on a sales technique known as "probing for the prospective customer's needs." Ask questions like:

"Is there any way that your interests are harmed by our conflict?"

"If our differences could be handled better (even if you feel this is not possible), how would you feel?"

"How would things be different for you if we were able to resolve this?"

This probing helps your Other recognize that she has something to gain by resolving the conflict.

Now to close the sale. The most powerful closing technique is simply asking the customer for the sale. You may say:

"I want to meet with you to talk this out, at a time and place convenient for you. Will you do that, please?"

In this "sales call" you help your Other identify some personal self-interests that are affected, and offer the hope that her needs might be satisfied. It is important in asking these questions that you not convey the impression that this is a manipulative strategy intended to help you and to hurt her. It is not a self-serving deception. You are simply choosing to assume that a both-gain solution is possible, and are inviting her to join you in this assumption. You, yourself, may have troubling doubts, but you are opting for optimism.

Few Commitments

Assure your Other that no commitments are requested except to:

- Tell you about her side of the situation.

- During this Dialogue, refrain from using intimidation, threat, or coercion to force a win-lose conclusion.

- Stay physically present and alert for an agreed-upon period of time.

Curiously, the Other need not trust that the meeting will be successful or productive, or even believe that any solution is possible other than agreeing to her previously stated demands. In fact, she is not required to acknowledge that there is a problem at all. You are only asking her to join you in a conversation dedicated to searching for agreement on issues of concern. There is little to lose, and potentially much to gain.

Take special care to get an explicit commitment from your Other that he WILL NOT WALK OUT until the time you have agreed to talk has expired, even if he feels further talk would be fruitless. This is an extremely important pre-condition. If one of you walks out on the other before the Breakthrough happens, then this meeting may be just another inflammatory argument. The commitment to stay for the predetermined time period is essential. The close of the meeting should occur only with mutual consent. If you cannot be certain that this fundamental requirement is met, then it may be risky to start the Dialogue.

Inflammatory language, personal insults, name-calling, and racial and ethnic slurs slow down progress. You can control your own language; you have less control over your Other's choice of words. If you feel vulnerable to being verbally abused, you may ask your Other to use restraint. Otherwise, hear his remarks as arising from the "heat of the moment" and try not to take personal offense.

Most simply, in finding a time to talk, you are asking the Other to join you in agreement-seeking Dialogue that is guided by the Cardinal Rules:

#1: DO NOT WITHDRAW

#2: DO NOT USE POWER-PLAYS

The page "Notes for the Other" (see p.203) is designed as a handout. You may wish to make a photocopy of it for your Other to help her understand your proposal.

Chapter 10:

Step 2
PLAN THE CONTEXT

The context is the time-and-place environment within which the Dialogue of Step 3 occurs. The purpose of planning the context is to create a setting for effective communication.

This chapter describes aspects of context that should be considered. Don't memorize the list. Just know where to turn in this book for quick reference while planning a meeting.

Location

A private place that is free from interruptions should be selected. Importantly, phone calls and people walking in should be prevented. Even music should be eliminated. Moving objects or people are visual distractions. The meeting should occur in a private room that other people will not inadvertently enter. A place where neither person feels on home turf, or a site preferred by your Other is best.

In most workplaces, Dialogues are best held in small conference rooms that can be reserved, or in vacant offices. Your or the Other's office is an alternative choice, if you are certain that interruptions can be prevented.

Physical Comforts

Discomforts distract. Arrange for comfortable seating, and consider temperature, lighting, and ventilation. Serving or eating food during the meeting is not advised, but you may want to have a pitcher of water nearby.

Duration

Note: This section conservatively assumes that you have not used the 4-Step Method previously with this particular Other, that your Other is not familiar with the Method and is somewhat reluctant to participate, and that the conflict is clearly a Clash, not a Blip. If you and your Other habitually abide by the Cardinal Rules during routine communication, then a special lengthy Dialogue may often be unnecessary.

Length of the Dialogue is a crucial factor. It is essential that enough time is available so that the Breakthrough can be reached. If this point of natural closure has not yet occurred when the agreed time period expires, then the meeting may not have helped.

Although some discussions require only a half-hour or less, it is often unwise to begin a Dialogue if you know that you will have to stop so soon. Two hours is usually more than enough. To be safe, you may wish to allot plenty of time.

It is helpful if both people have realistic expectations about the meeting. Each should understand that most of the time in discussion may be spent in frustrating struggle. The Breakthrough and the deal-making that follow take only a short time, but the difficult and often discouraging effort that precedes it is a necessary part of the journey. You must know this fact and trust its truth, even if your Other does not.

Quitting the Dialogue before its positive conclusion is the most common cause of failure in using the 4-Step Method. If you are at all doubtful about the strength of your resolve to stay in stressful confrontation with your Other long enough to reach the Breakthrough (that is, your commitment to Cardinal Rule #1), then I urge you to carefully read Part 4 of this book. The behavioral science explanations for why this persistence pays off may be reassuring.

Confidentiality

The privacy of things you both say in this meeting should be respected. Rumors only inflame conflict and undermine success.

The agreement you make may become an announced job activity that is known to colleagues. Also, the fact that the two of you have met to discuss a problem may become common knowledge among co-workers. Still, details of the discussion leading up to the deal-making need not be disclosed.

As the initiator of this Method, you have direct control only over your own part in maintaining confidentiality. You can do little to influence your Other's behavior beyond requesting that he afford you the same consideration. If you are unsure about his ability or willingness to do this, you may want to be especially mindful of what you disclose during the Dialogue.

Interruptions

Absolutely none! Make arrangements to have incoming phone calls intercepted by a secretary, or answered by a telephone answering machine. Also, arrange to avoid interruptions by colleagues who might walk in unannounced.

Timing

The time of day or time of week can affect energy level, attentiveness, and distractibility during your discussion. The rule of thumb is: "Find a time when you both are not or preoccupied with other concerns."

Who Else Is Present?

No one.

Chapter 11:

Step 3
TALK IT OUT

Meeting to talk is the core ingredient of the 4-Step Method. Steps one and two just make the meeting happen. Performing your two tasks within the recommended structure and context of the discussion releases energy that is bound up in conflict. Releasing this energy produces a shift in attitudes from me-against-you to us-against-the-problem—the "Breakthrough."

The Structure

The meeting consists of four parts: The Opening, the Invitation, the Dialogue, and the Breakthrough. Let's flesh out the skeleton with examples of how each part may be performed.

The OPENING

EXPRESS APPRECIATION

"I appreciate your willingness to meet with me to talk this out."

EXPRESS OPTIMISM

"I'm hopeful that we can find a solution that is beneficial to both of us."

REMINDERS (The Cardinal Rules)

"It's very important that our discussion is not interrupted, and that we don't give up or walk out, even if we get frustrated. Are you certain you can be here until 4:00 if we need to be?

"Also, let's agree for this meeting to refrain from using Power-plays to defeat the other. Instead, let's look for solutions that both might accept. OK?"

STATE THE ISSUE

"My understanding of the issue is that we have different views about what my role is in the Atlantic Project."

The INVITATION

"Please tell me how you see the situation."

The DIALOGUE

During the Dialogue, which consumes most of the time in the meeting, you perform two tasks:

- Keeping both you and your Other actively engaged in face-to-face communication (the Essential Process).

- Supporting conciliatory gestures* made by the Other, and offering them yourself when you can do so sincerely.

Let's take a closer look at how these tasks are performed.

---

*   Defined as "uncoerced behaviors, typically verbal, that display vulnerability to one's opponent in conflict." Also see Chapter 20 for a fuller explanation of conciliatory gestures.

The Essential Process

The "Essential Process" is the form of communication that is required to effectively manage interpersonal differences and resolve conflict:

Face-to-face talking

about the issues on which we differ

without interruption

for as long as necessary

to reach the "Breakthrough"

You have initiated the 4-Step Method and understand its purpose; your Other may not have this understanding. So it is up to you to maintain the process. Typical lapses in the Essential Process include:

- Talking about subjects that are not relevant to your relationship (weather, current events, technical information, other safe topics)

- Talking about other people (co-workers, senior management, other departments) as if they hold the only key to solving your problem

- Telling jokes

- Giving up, expressing hopelessness

- Falling silent

When your Other engages in these diversionary behaviors, revive the Essential Process with your next comment. Redirecting, rather than critizing, is more helpful.

Illustrations:

"Let's get back to the problem at hand. How do you feel about . . . "

"I know it seems hopeless, but let's see if we can find a way out of this."

"You've been quiet awhile. I'd like to hear about what you are thinking."

Emotional readiness to let go of prior demands comes partly from the catharsis of talking. Give your Other plenty of opportunity to express opinions, views, feelings, and judgments. Think of your job description as: "To solicit the Other's views on the issues." Listen with as much patience and interest as you can muster.

Of course, much of what your Other says, especially early in the Dialogue, may be difficult for you to hear. She may criticize and blame you, make statements that you feel are unfair or factually incorrect, and repeat old arguments that have angered you in the past. Feeling assaulted by these comments may incite you to retaliate. After all, you, too, are only human, and may feel as much resentment toward your Other as she may be feeling toward you. Like her, you need time to talk and express your side. You also need to ventilate your pent-up frustrations. If you are confident that your Other will not renege on her commitment to the Cardinal Rules, you can express your anger openly.

Conciliatory Gestures

With time (though not as quickly as you might like) you may expect friendly comments, or "conciliatory gestures" to appear. The Other's remarks will begin to reveal a slackening of "me-against-you" energy that drives his need to fight. This signals you that he is becoming more receptive to an "us-against-the-problem" orientation toward the problem. Genuine, sincere conciliatory gestures do not occur until aggressive impulses have been somewhat spent through catharsis and ventilation.

Since you are the one who is managing the Dialogue, it is your job to be alert to the Other's friendly comments. When she expresses a conciliatory gesture, even if you are still angry, try to acknowledge it.

Illustration:

"I appreciate your telling me that you regret saying what you did in the staff meeting last week. I'm still upset about the impression it left about me with the vice-president."

Your support of the Other's friendly comments will encourage her to make similar comments later. These conciliatory gestures help move you toward the Breakthrough.

Do Not Score Points

Conciliatory gestures always place the person offering them in a vulnerable position. His Other is presented with an opportunity to take advantage of the open, non-defensive comment to "score a point."

When the Other offers a conciliatory gesture, you should not yield to the temptation to score. *Do not take advantage of your Other's vulnerability*, even if he takes advantage of yours. Rejecting the Other's efforts to conciliate is a common retaliatory tactic used during ordinary arguments. But doing so damages trust and widens the gap to be bridged. The Dialogue is a special opportunity, not an ordinary argument. For many people, scoring points may be an old bad habit; try not to do it.

This process prevents both you and your Other from indulging in the false safety and familiarity of the Wrong Reflexes. It helps you replace these destructive patterns of behavior with the Cardinal Rules for constructive engagement.

The BREAKTHROUGH

Performing these two tasks—staying in the Essential Process, and supporting conciliatory gestures—in this context creates conditions in which voluntary, uncoerced agreement can occur. The Breakthrough happens when you and the Other shift from me-against-you fighting to an us-against-the-problem search for solutions.

On most occasions some agreement, even if limited, can be reached in one Dialogue. If for any reason one meeting does not produce the Breakthrough, DO NOT GIVE UP. Schedule another time to talk within the next few days, or even better if within a few hours. Don't let this setback squelch your optimism that a way can be found around the boulder in the road.

Often, the passage of a brief period of time after an unsuccessful Dialogue actually allows a face-saving opportunity to make concessions. After a time-break, conciliatory gestures can be justified by "having had a chance to think it over." In reality, thinking it over may have had little to do with the shift in attitude. Nevertheless, the shift will have occurred and agreement reached.

The Spearcatcher Strategy

When using the 4-Step Method, it can be helpful to think of yourself as a "spearcatcher." The spearcatcher realizes that no actual harm can come from "word spears" and so allows them to strike without self-defensive maneuvering. She fearlessly lets verbal slings and arrows hail down, and is shielded by the knowledge that words can do no physical harm. The spearcatcher actually invites spears when she senses the Other is withholding ammunition. Although in battle, she is safe in knowing that accepting the Other's attack without retaliating is a secret strategy for eliciting a more compromising attitude from the Other.

The spearcatcher stifles the impulse to retaliate. Although she feels the impulse to react, she does not act on it—she exercises willpower over her own behavior. She presents herself as an available target for the Other's attacks, knowing that his aggressive energy will eventually become spent. Then, when the Other is in a more receptive mood, she can negotiate a beneficial agreement.

Illustrations:

"How did you feel after I broke my promise?"

"What did you think about me when you found out I was the one who wrote the critical memo?"

Caution!

Except when both you and your Other are fully knowledgeable about the spearcatcher variation of the 4-Step Method, I do not advise its use with business partners or your closest work associates.

Why? In relationships with those closest to us, we wish to enhance trust and openness. Synergy and joint creativity require these characteristics. In contrast, our goal in relation to many co-workers, bosses, and subordinates is simply to be able to work together cooperatively in performing our jobs—deep trust and openness is not necessary or desired.

By its nature, spearcatching is a deceptive manipulation. It speeds up the emergence of conciliatory gestures from your Other, but tricks him into believing that your receptiveness and apparent openness to his arguments are genuine. In truth, your acquiescence is not entirely sincere. It is highly unlikely that you will have been convinced by your Other's argument that he is right and that you are wrong. By neglecting to defend yourself, you are allowing him to make a false assumption. You are permitting him to think that you have conceded some points (called "bargaining chips") in order to shape his emotional state into a less defensive form that will more likely lead to concessions on the issues that are of real interest to you. Using spearcatching regularly as a secret strategy with close workmates can erode trust and promote dishonest relationships.

A Better Way

By staying in problem-focused conversation, we act as if there were a both-gain solution, rather than allowing the Win- Lose Illusion to control us. Assuming that only win-lose outcomes are possible leads to Non-communication and Power-play strategies. The both-gain assumption permits a mutually satisfactory solution to be found whenever possible; assuming it is a win-or-lose situation that precludes this possibility.

So we recognize that there is an alternative to the Wrong Reflexes that all too often keep conflicts unresolved. The alternative is staying in process—keeping communication happening. The passage of time in uninterrupted communication eventually permits the forces harnessed by the 4-Step Method to bring harmony to discordant working relationships.

Chapter 12:

SKILLS FOR DIALOGUE

The 4-Step Method overcomes the most typical obstacles to interpersonal agreement: The Wrong Reflexes. Simply engaging in face-to-face conversation in the appropriate context while complying with the Cardinal Rules helps people manage their differences and build more satisfying and productive relationships.

But the skeptical reader is asking, "What about skills? Aren't special skills needed in the Dialogue?"

How old are you? You have that many years' experience in the school of life. You have learned more than you may realize about how to communicate, about how to get along with others. Of course, we also learn ineffective communication patterns along with more positive skills. But, on balance, most adults who are able to maintain friendships, hold jobs, join groups, and survive the crucible of family life possess sufficient communication skills to make the 4-Step Method work.

Still, let's not ignore the contributions of the applied behavioral sciences that can enhance our ability to use the 4- Step Method successfully. Three social skills are especially helpful: *Listening, Negotiation,* and *Assertiveness.*

LISTENING

If talking and listening are the two acts of verbal communication, listening is the nobler half.

Listening demonstrates openness to what the Other is saying. How can this receptivity be communicated during the Dialogue? Here are some specific listening tools:

- Keeping steady eye contact
- Not interrupting
- Not giving advice

- Summarizing what you have heard

- Making reflective statements, showing that you understand how the Other feels

Hostile enemies don't listen. Using these listening tools conveys to the Other that you are not a hostile enemy, and that you are open to considering his needs and concerns. Sensing that his needs are respected, your Other will be less motivated to escalate his aggressiveness in order to drive his points home to you. By listening, you are demonstrating that you are not hiding behind the impenetrable shield of sealed ears, but are open and receptive to the Other. You are willing to hear.

NEGOTIATION

We get our needs met by others through negotiation. Some popular writers have equated negotiation with "power bargaining" in which the needs of the Other are not considered. But here we are concerned with managing differences in ongoing interdependent workplace relationships. Our needs are mutual and reciprocal. Power bargaining erodes trust and goodwill. Such a strategy is short-sighted at best, and self-destructive at worst.

A better model for the Dialogue is "principled negotiation"* which consists of four basic guidelines for interaction. To the extent that we can behave according to these principles during the Dialogue, the more effective the 4-Step Method will be in producing agreement.

---

* Adapted from Roger Fisher and William Ury, *Getting to Yes*. Boston: Houghton Mifflin, 1981.

1) *Separate the PERSON from the PROBLEM.*

Certain characteristics of your Other may annoy you. Her values may offend you. His mannerisms may irritate you. As much as you might wish these characteristics to change, they will not. Your Other will remain the same person with much the same psychological make-up, despite your rehabilitative efforts on his behalf. Furthermore, criticizing personal characteristics will only inflame the conflict by arousing defenses. So how can the situation change? Happily, the conflict can be resolved without changing the person. Do your best to avoid discussing personal characteristics, either your own or your Other's. Focus instead on the problem—the issues on which agreement or joint action is sought.

2) *Focus on INTERESTS, not POSITIONS.*

Conflicts happen in part because disputants hold (apparently) incompatible positions on one or more issues. To paraphrase songwriter Paul Simon's melodious commentary on this dilemma, "You want to work with the window open, I want to work with the window closed. Goodbye, goodbye, goodbye." Here, the issue in contention is whether the window should be open or closed while they work. The diametrically opposed positions that the two workmates hold seem to have lead to one's quitting his job—an interpersonal and organizational tragedy.

The trap of debating positions is that the best possible solution is a splitting-the-difference compromise. The essence of compromise is that neither disputant gets what she wants. Position-based bargaining is a win-lose power struggle.

But every position put forth by disputants rests on underlying self-interests that may be unclear even to oneself. If instead of argu-

ing about positions we probe for our own and the other's underlying self-interests, then both-gain alternatives may come into view.
"How does working with the window closed affect me?" "What do
you like about working with the window open?" By exploring the
answers to these questions, it becomes conceivable that both
disputants' self-interests may be satisfied, and that neither must lose.

3) *Invent OPTIONS for mutual gain.*

Interest-based bargaining promotes a less contentious climate
in the Dialogue that aids the search for both-gain solutions. In this
more collaborative mode, you may search creatively for alternatives
that might benefit both of you. Now the Dialogue is a problem-
solving discussion where your orientation is us-against-the-problem
rather than me-against-you. Ideally, both disputants can brainstorm
possible solutions, listing as many ideas as you can think of without
worrying about how practical or promising they are. Once a pool of
alternative solutions has been brainstormed, each option can be
tested for compatibility with each disputant's underlying self-
interests.

4) *Identify objective CRITERIA.*

To agree on an issue is to make a joint decision. Decisions are
always based on criteria for judging whether they are good or bad
decisions.

In typical arguments (searches for a joint decision), these
criteria are generally not conscious or explicit. But just because we
are not aware of them doesn't mean decision criteria are not
present. Let's say you have decided to take your new co-worker to
Tony's Pizzaria for lunch rather than Wong's Rice Kitchen. How

did you make that decision? If you answer, "Because the food is better" or "Because the atmosphere is better," then we now know that the criterion for the decision about where to eat lunch was "The food must be good" or "The atmosphere must be pleasant." That is, a good decision must meet these criteria. A bad decision would fail to meet these criteria, and you would regret your restaurant selection.

An objective criterion is neutral with respect to the self- interests of the disputants. That is, an unbiased observer would say that your agreement is a fair one. If the criteria for agreement between you and your Other are objective, rather than subjective, then your agreement is more stable and likely to last. If criteria are subjective, then one disputant will feel that the decision was unfair and therefore will not feel motivated to implement it.

Return to our conflict over working with the window open or closed. An objective criterion for deciding what to do about the problem might be: "Both people have the right to work comfortably." Therefore, a fair solution will permit each person to work comfortably. An agreement (joint decision) that satisfies that criterion will be a good one.

ASSERTIVENESS

If I could grant my children only one social skill, it would be assertiveness.

Let's define what we mean by this often misunderstood idea. It is best understood as one of three social behaviors taken together:

Aggression: Behavior that violates another person's rights.

Submission: Behavior that allows another person to violate one's rights.

Assertion: Behavior that insists on one's own rights without violating the rights of others.

Readers who are familiar with certain Asian cultures will recognize that, at least in hierarchical organizations, submission to superiors is necessary to survival. To behave assertively risks causing loss of face to the superior, and promptly leads to social ostracism of the assertive person. Within a Western cultural context, however, I assert the following two value judgments:

- *Assertiveness is good difference-managing behavior.*
- *Aggressiveness and submissiveness are poor difference-managing behaviors.*

Aggressiveness sparks defensiveness in others. Also, aggressiveness is its behavioral expression—the way we act when we feel defensive. Submissiveness may be a useful short-term strategy to avoid confrontation, but it sows the seeds for resentments that flower into future episodes of conflict.

Again illustrating with the open/closed window conflict, the workmate who slams down the window and shouts threateningly at the Other to leave it down is behaving aggressively. The Other's rights to have his comfort considered have been violated. If the workmate who was shouted at gives up the struggle and works poorly because of the stuffy air, he is behaving submissively. This workmate, having his rights violated, will surely feel resentful. This state of affairs does not promote good teamwork.

An alternative to submissiveness is assertiveness: "I want to work comfortably—cooling ventilation would help me do that." By stating one's needs and insisting that they be considered by the Other, one is more likely to find a mutually acceptable solution on the issue. Even if a both-gain solution is not found, one can more willingly accept a less-than-ideal solution without holding a residue of hostility, ready to burst out in response to the next triggering event.

Bumpy, but a Road Nonetheless

So listening, asserting your needs, and negotiating on principle in the Dialogue will help you reach the Breakthrough. Even if your skills in these areas are highly developed, you will find the road bumpy. There exists no smooth avenue to agreement when differences are great. Those of us with more yet to learn must abide the ruts and potholes. Just do your best with the skills you have gained in the school of life. The road may be rough, but it leads to where you want to go.

Chapter 13:

Step 4
MAKE A DEAL

For many people, the most surprising part of the 4-Step Method is the Breakthrough, the shift in attitude from me- against-you to us-against-the-problem. Defensiveness, mistrust, and vengefulness lift like morning fog from the interpersonal battlefield, revealing possible routes around the Boulder in the Road. Both you and your Other are now psychologically ready to join efforts in mutually searching for the best route.

Why does the Breakthrough happen? Ironically, it does not result from logical persuasion, rational thinking, or reasonable problem-solving, although we may think so at the time. Instead, it springs automatically from several psychological forces that converge to produce this significant but often unnoticed event. Chapter 20 will discuss these forces.

The Breakthrough opens a window of opportunity in which both participants are willing to agree about something. Together, you can take advantage of this mutual openness to agree about a disputed workplace issue. More than producing goodwill, a Deal prescribes how you will interact with one another in the future. The most successful agreements are *balanced, behaviorally specific,* and *written.*

BALANCED

Often, a Deal consists of an exchange of concessions from each person—"I'll do this if you'll do that." At other times, a creative both-gain solution can be found that satisfies each participant's needs while requiring no concessions from either.

Whether a dramatic discovery of similar underlying self- interests, or a fair compromise involving concessions, the Deal should be balanced. That is, each person should gain a personal benefit from the Deal. Their gains need not be exactly equal, but the Deal should give each person an incentive for doing her part in the future. An unbalanced agreement is a short-lived agreement.

BEHAVIORALLY SPECIFIC

The Deal captures in specific behavior the spirit of goodwill present at the Breakthrough.

Agreements that are too general or that focus on our thoughts, attitudes, or values can fail because we can't see or hear thoughts, attitudes, and values. These "mental events" are invisible, hidden inside our heads. Agreements about behaviors that can be seen or heard are verifiable.

For example, your agreement to "respect my wishes" or "be honest" may unravel because we cannot verify whether you are in fact "respecting my wishes" or "being honest." You may claim that you are; I may feel that you are not. Intentions are not as easy to discern as behaviors.

So we should frame agreements that are specific as to who is to do what, by when, for how long, under what conditions. If a Deal is behaviorally specific, it will be easy to determine how fully each person has lived up to it.

During the Deal-making part of the Dialogue, it is helpful to test proposed parts of the agreement for behavioral specificity. Useful questions to ask:

"How will I be able to tell that you are [respecting my wishes]?"

"What behaviors will I see and hear if you are [being honest]?"

The result will be a clear mutual understanding of how the Deal will be carried out. If you are deciding which of you is to make the sales trip to Kansas City, all compromises and concessions are detailed. If you are defining responsibilities in the Atlantic project, all aspects of your interdependent roles will be described. This clarity results in a separation of your responsibilities from my responsibilities in solving our problem.

WRITTEN

Normally, agreements are more complicated than simple yes-or-no decisions or other easy-to-remember solutions. Recording Deals in mutually acceptable terms will help protect against selective memory loss in the future. Each person should keep copies of the written document. Sometimes questions arise in the future about what was in fact agreed to. The written document is objective evidence that can help answer such questions.

Personal Responsibility

No Deal will work unless each person accepts individual responsibility for doing her part. The usual challenge to people struggling with differences is how to separate my responsibilities from yours in solving our problem. Using the 4-Step Method solves that dilemma—a behaviorally specific agreement separates each person's responsibilities from the other's.

Once the agreement is described in behavioral detail, it is then up to each person to fulfill the responsibility that is uniquely and clearly hers—a much easier challenge. Once a Deal has been created that serves each one's self-interests, both people have an incentive to responsibly perform their parts.

Limiting the Duration of the Deal

It may be helpful to agree in advance to limit the length of time that the agreement will be in force. That is, you may prefer to commit to it for only one week or one month. At the end of that time, you may wish to renegotiate parts of the agreement. Until that time, you should obligate yourself to doing what you have agreed to do, even if it begins to feel unfair or unsatisfactory after awhile.

Is a Deal Always Necessary?

Much of the Dialogue's value is simply in opening lines of communication. Although words can hurt, face-to-face communication is also a healing and restorative medicine for wounded relationships. So, the particular items of agreement may be of only secondary importance.

This is especially true of managing differences between close colleagues and business partners. In fact, Step 4 may be ignored entirely when there is no problem to solve—just "talk it out" occasionally to renew trust and mutual respect.

Often, however, a decision about a joint course of action must be made and implemented, such as selecting the salesperson to make that trip to Kansas City next week. Typically, workplace conflicts involve business problems that demand solution. In these instances, the Breakthrough presents an important opportunity to make a Deal about a problem that requires an answer.

The Bottom Line

The question of whether making a Deal is necessary reduces to this:

- If a decision or course of action related to the contested issue requires the consent or involvement of both persons, then a Deal must be made.

- If not, concluding the Dialogue with an agreement is optional. Still, doing so may help participants feel a satisfying sense of closure.

SAMPLE AGREEMENT

Situation: Donna manages a data processing service unit in a financial services company. Lowell is the most experienced programmer-analyst in the unit, and is uniquely qualified to answer many technical questions from users. Donna is an experienced manager, and is not as technically skilled as Lowell. As a result, Donna often interrupts Lowell to ask questions, and Lowell gets angry about being distracted while concentrating intensely on his programming.

Issue: How can Donna get technical information from Lowell that meets her need for prompt service to users, and yet does not interrupt his concentration at critical times while programming.

Donna agrees to:
1) Judge whether a request for information must be answered today, or can wait until tomorrow.

2) When it must be answered today, she will quietly put a written note at a designated place on Lowell's desk requesting his time.

3) When it can be answered tomorrow, she will hold the question until a regularly scheduled meeting between herself and Lowell at 4:30 each day.

Benefit for Donna: She gets prompt answers to her most urgent questions.

Lowell agrees to:
1) Not openly question Donna's judgment about the urgency of needed answers.

2) Respond to Donna's written notes on his next break, or sooner if he can interrupt his programming.

3) Be prepared to meet with Donna at 4:30 each day to answer the less urgent questions.

Benefit for Lowell: His concentration is not interrupted during critical programming activities.

We agree to abide by this agreement until we talk again next week. At that time, we will assess how the agreement has been working, and may modify and improve it as needed.

Use It or Lose It

This completes our description of the 4-Step Method for managing interpersonal differences at work. Try it. Do the best you can. Don't be reluctant to use it because you don't think you understand it well enough. The Method is robust. It tolerates mistakes and imperfections. Just keep in mind the most vital ingredient, the Essential Process:

Face-to-face talking

about the issues on which we differ

without interruption

for as long as necessary

to reach the Breakthrough

In the Dialogue, act how you choose to act, not how you feel like acting. Choice requires courage more than skill.

Practice using it. After one or two successes, your guidance for future uses of the 4-Step Method will come from your own knowledge—not from the words in this book.

Chapter 14:

MEDIATION: HELPING OTHERS MANAGE THEIR DIFFERENCES

The 4-Step Method for constructive difference-management has evolved through my work as a mediator since the mid-1960's. I define mediation as:

"The role of a neutral third party in facilitating the search for mutually acceptable, self-determined agreements between two or more disputants."

This chapter examines how the simple 4-Step Method can be used by managers and other third parties in helping others manage their differences.

The Active-Passive Debate

In mediation, as in other professional fields, practitioners disagree. One debate among mediators concerns how active or passive the mediator should be during meetings with disputants. That is, does success depend on the substantive contributions of the mediator (the "active mediator" argument)? Or, does success arise from factors other than the mediator's expert knowledge about the substantive issues in dispute (the "passive mediator" argument)? If a combination, in what proportion do these two elements contribute to success in finding solutions?

An important consideration in the active-passive debate is the "structure" of the parties. Structure refers to

- the size of the parties—whether they are individuals, groups, or organizations;

- the number of separate contesting parties; and

- the degree of consensus of opinion within each party that permits it to speak with one voice through a leader or representative.

Method Fits Simplest Structure

Forms of mediation are used in negotiating agreements to complex problems, such as labor contract disputes and corporate strategic plans involving several department heads. Mediation is also used with two individuals, such as co-workers and business partners. Clearly, the two-person relationship has the most simple structure possible.

The 4-Step Method as described up to this point may be thought of as "self-mediation," although this is technically a contradiction in terms since we defined mediation as a *third*-party role. The Method calls for one participant to initiate the Dialogue and perform certain functions that are normally done by a neutral third party. The rules of the process act as the mediator.

The 4-Step Method can be simple because it is designed specifically for managing differences only in two-person relationships. Applying the Method to more complex situations calls for careful attention to the implications of other structural features.

Where Does Resolution Come From?

Now, back to the active-passive debate. The argument reduces to this basic question: "Are the forces that lead to resolution of interpersonal conflict introduced by the mediator, or do they exist within the pair relationship itself?" If the mediator produces the resolution, then the forces are external to the pair—this would require active mediation. If the resolution evolves as a natural product of communication between the parties under the special environment that mediation provides, then the forces are internal to the pair—this would permit passive mediation.

My experience, as well as substantial research and theory in behavioral science, suggests that passive mediation is effective when structure is simple, and is ineffective when structure is complex. That is, the forces that lead to resolution of two-person conflicts are latent in the relationship between the partners, ready to come forth when conditions are favorable. Mediation is an opportunity for structured communication that allows those forces to emerge and take effect. These are described in detail in Chapter 20: "Forces Toward Harmony."

ROLE OF THE MEDIATOR

So, we conclude that passive mediation is effective in resolving two-person conflicts. Since we recognize that the Method can produce interpersonal agreements without a third party, you might be wondering, "Of what use, then, is a mediator?"

A mediator can perform several useful functions that help the Method achieve more satisfactory results than when it is used as self-mediation:

1) A reluctant disputant can be more effectively persuaded to participate if the Dialogue is proposed by a third party than if proposed by her opponent. The mistrustful climate of most interpersonal conflicts leads one to suspect that her Other is driven by manipulative, self-serving motives in suggesting that they meet to discuss contested issues. When proposed by a neutral mediator who has no personal stake in the outcome other than that an agreement be reached, this suspiciousness and distrust is minimized.

2) The mediator can exercise more control in ensuring that a participant who becomes frustrated with the Method will not break Cardinal Rule #1 by withdrawing or walking out. When the Dialogue is under way with no mediator, the per-

son who has initiated it is vulnerable to his Other's reneging on the commitment to stay in the meeting until it is concluded. A mediator can more forcefully insist that a wavering participant stay in the room and continue discussion.

3) The mediator can exercise more control in ensuring that neither disputant violates Cardinal Rule #2 by employing coercive force or intimidating threats to defeat her foe. Indeed, some lopsided power conflicts may be resolvable only through mediation.

4) The mediator, being less emotionally involved, can listen more attentively for conciliatory gestures. When such a gesture occurs, the mediator can bring attention to it with a comment like "It sounded like you made an offer to compromise a moment ago. Could you say more about that?" or "Did you notice that Susan said she felt bad for you?" This kind of supportive attention can be difficult for a participant to give, especially when he is angry.

5) When the Breakthrough occurs, the mediator can more effectively help frame an agreement than if deal-making is left to the disputants. The mediator may be able to think more clearly about the necessary elements of a behaviorally specific agreement than can a participant who remains emotionally upset. Also, urgings by a mediator to correct a flaw in an agreement are met with less defensive resistance than when weak spots are noted by a foe.

6) Finally, a mediator can make use of what social psychologists call the "audience effect" in following up with participants at some agreed time in the future. The audience effect accounts for why participants feel more obligated to

a neutral third party in living up to their part of an agreement than they do to their counterpart in conflict. Follow-up by the mediator typically consists of

- Meeting again with the participants at a specific time agreed to by all at the close of the Dialogue.

- Asking at the follow-up meeting, "How is it working?" to prompt the participants to review the agreement.

- Helping to fine-tune the agreement if necessary.

- Congratulating the people on their successful efforts to improve their relationship.

WHO CAN MEDIATE?

The 4-Step Method is generic; it can be used to resolve any two-person conflict that meets the prerequisites in Chapter 17. The only requirements of the mediator who manages the Method are that she

- is accepted by both participants into the third-party role. This acceptance is most likely when the mediator is perceived by each one as

- relatively neutral and unbiased, meaning that she is not an advocate of either person, and

- having some base of power to enter the role of third-party with the two people in conflict. This power can reside in either

  - being perceived as a competent mediator, or

  - having authority to require that a Dialogue occur, even if one or both participants are reluctant to meet.

- refrain from interfering with the Essential Process during the Dialogue. Mediators are best able to avoid this common mistake who

  - know the procedure of the 4-Step Method,
  - understand some of the behavioral science that explains how the Method produces the Breakthrough, and
  - have confidence that the Method works.

Low-Skill Mediation?

Many people are surprised by how little skill and knowledge are required of the mediator. Surprise may arise from the popular belief that the mediator's personal abilities account for more of the results of mediation than is argued here.

On a cautionary note, however, I recommend that you at least be experienced in using the 4-Step Method in "self-mediation" before undertaking a third-party effort. Although it is simple to understand, pitfalls can trip the new mediator that only experience can teach her to avoid. I am reminded of the saying, "Good judgment comes from experience; experience comes from bad judgment." Give yourself several opportunities to practice bad judgment in self-mediation before offering your good judgment to others.

If you are now a mediator who holds different assumptions about your role than are presented here, I do not expect you to be persuaded so readily that some of your favorite mediation tools are less than vital. And, please remember that the 4-Step Method is designed for self-help, not for professional service. I do not suggest that more complex and demanding mediation tools may not be helpful and at times required. Mediators are invited to test this simple model and report their experiences to me c/o the publisher.

Figure 9:
Matching mediation method to the structure of the parties.

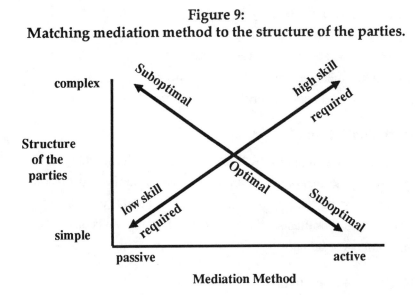

FORMS OF MEDIATION

As long as the basic mediator requirements mentioned above are met, then mediators can assist pairs of people wherever they find them. The 4-Step Method can help people manage differences and build better working relationships throughout the organization.

Managerial Mediation

I have been involved since 1979 in developing and promoting managerial mediation as a new form of participative management. Increasingly, managers are using mediation to solve productivity problems resulting from poor communication and cooperation between employees—estimated to account for 65% of job performance deficiency.

Managers hold a significant advantage, compared with mediators who are not in roles of authority. If necessary, the manager can override employees' reluctance to participate by pointing to the impact on productivity resulting from their difficulty in working cooperatively. Because the managerial mediation session is a business meeting, not a discussion of personal issues, it is a powerful means of solving organizational problems.

Staff Mediation

Here, a staff employee performs mediation with two other employees who are not his subordinates. Typical staff mediators are personnel specialists, employee relations staff, internal organization development consultants, employee assistance program counselors, and training consultants.

Mediation Consultancy

Increasingly, behavioral science-based consultants are serving their organizational clients by helping key individuals enhance trust and cooperation through mediation.

A Better Way

The field of mediation has grown tremendously since 1980. Modern organizations are discovering that there is a better way to resolve conflicts than the means that we have relied upon throughout history. Although forms of third-party intervention in disputes have existed for centuries, the need has never been greater than now for constructive ways to manage human differences in organizational life.

PART 3

Chapter 15:

RESOLUTION IS NON-RATIONAL

The problem does not have to be solved for the conflict to be resolved.

"Hogwash!" you exclaim. "That doesn't make sense!" Let's take a closer look.

Many people find it surprising that the path to harmonious teamwork winds through a jungle where anger, resentment, and similar "negative" feelings flourish. You have noticed that the 4-Step Method does not discourage the expression of these feelings—it permits their ventilation. This contradicts popular admonitions to "put on a happy face" and "be logical."

A Lesson from Psychology

One of the most common tasks of psychotherapists is to help clients become aware of their repressed anger, and to aid them in learning to express it in nondestructive, nonviolent, healthy ways in appropriate situations. Seldom do therapists find it suitable to help their clients suppress angry feelings. Repressed anger is a major cause of neurosis, particularly depression, and poisons interpersonal relationships.

The "Talk It Out" step of the 4-Step Method provides a structured, relatively safe opportunity for the productive expression of anger. This is necessary. We must go through, not around. Finding interpersonal harmony requires ventilation without violence, contact without withdrawal.

Reason and Emotion

Conflict is not resolved by reason alone. In fact, reasonableness has little to do with it. Still, our rational minds recoil at such an irrational notion.

When embroiled in conflicts with co-workers, we strive to achieve:

- solutions to the disputed issues, and

- enhancement of mutual trust and respect, and the overall climate of cooperativeness.

Only when people don't need much from each other (low inter-dependency) can their differences be adequately managed by reaching rational agreement on substantive issues. Conflicts that occur in our most important workplace relationships involve fundamental questions of trust, respect, and cooperativeness. These are deeply emotional, not rational. Distrust is not amenable to rational solution.

Therefore, our first goal in using the Method is to produce an emotional climate of trust, acceptance, and cooperativeness. Once such a climate is achieved, disagreements on substantive issues can be more easily solved in mutually satisfactory ways. And, perhaps just as importantly, differences on sticky, persistent issues can be managed without destroying trust.

No Perfect Solution

Unfortunately, a single use of the 4-Step Method cannot "fix" a relationship. Changes in the emotional climate that are produced by one Dialogue are seldom permanent. This may be disappointing, since we all hope for permanent solutions. The inescapable, unhappy fact is that no such solutions exist in human relationships.

So, in the real world, it is more accurate to say that our differences are "managed" than to say our conflicts are "resolved."

Trust the Process

Recognizing this fact, we must abandon the unrealistic expectation that we solve our conflicts rationally.

Paradoxically, we must entrust ourselves to a process over which we cannot have direct control, and which may not even make rational sense to us. Accepting that we cannot force the outcome we want, we must trust the process to bring it to us.

On Accepting Discomfort

Perhaps someone with the self-discipline of a Zen master is able to become emotionally detached enough to not feel uncomfortable during Dialogue. The rest of us mortals don't have such control over our emotions; we find conflict unpleasant. The 4-Step Method requires that we deal with the Other face-to-face, and tolerate a tense, charged atmosphere while talking it out. The Method is simple, but perhaps not emotionally easy. Using it calls on us to accept being temporarily uncomfortable. We must make a conscious decision in advance to withstand momentary discomfort in order to accomplish our objective of improved communication with our Other.

With practice, the knowledge that you are acting choicefully and purposefully, accompanied by your growing confidence that the 4-Step Method actually works, will diminish the discomfort you feel. Still, the meeting may be stressful. Using this communication tool requires courage in tolerating discomfort, not skill in avoiding it.

Chapter 16:

WHAT IT CAN DO, WHAT IT CAN'T

In my practice of organizational mediation, I encounter a frequently held wish—people want conflict to vanish.

This desire for peace is surely understandable, but it can lead to trouble. If unchecked, the hope for conflict to disappear brings the expectation that if mediation is successful, my client's relationship will be free of conflict in the future. If that is my mission, I am doomed to failure.

A Fantasy

Our fantasy is that conflict should be absent in "good" business relationships. We regard conflict as a social disease, and assume that there must be a cure.

We seem to relish this idealistic fantasy, and suffer disappointment repeatedly as the plague of conflict infects our important workplace relationships. We seem unable to grasp the fact that conflict is as inherent to relationships as "wet" is to water. When pressed, we may grudgingly acknowledge that conflict is part of the package we buy when we join with others in interdependency. But a quiet interlude causes the fantasy to rise again like a phoenix from the ashes of interpersonal war. Beware of its return. Take note:

The 4-Step Method cannot cure conflict.

Clinging to the impossible dream of a conflict-free relationship with your colleague, boss, or subordinate may jeopardize your ability to use the 4-Step Method effectively. Holding up that fantasy as a gauge for measuring success, you will always be disappointed. You might reject whatever gains you achieve because they don't match your expectations. Do not repeat the folly of the hungry fisherman who throws back a small catch in disgust because it would not fill his skillet. Take nourishment even from small portions and imperfect successes.

So the question for this chapter is not, "Why is conflict inevitable?" Let us accept that truism as an unwelcome fact of life. Rather, let's consider the question, "What can I realistically expect to gain by using the 4-Step Method for managing differences?"

Again: Relationships and Needs

Let's revisit the metaphor introduced in Chapter 1 that views relationships as vehicles for the satisfaction of partners' needs. Each of us has needs that we look to the Other to satisfy; our relationship is the vehicle that transports these needs. The more needs the vehicle must carry, the greater the weight of its load. Sometimes, the weight exceeds the vehicle's strength.

Even strong relationships have limits. When the vehicle is overburdened, some needs don't get met. Further, they are weakened when time for communication is insufficient. Co-workers who are facing deadlines, employees who are busy with their jobs, bosses who have other obligations than supporting our work—these other activities squeeze out the time and energy available for communication. They are loads that weigh down the vehicle of our relationship so that little is left for attending to our needs. When the vehicle is loaded to capacity, we have nothing left to give.

When partners' needs of the Other overload the vehicle's ability to carry them, then some needs remain unmet. Consequently, one may feel unsupported in the relationship. It is a short step from feeling unsupported to feeling resentful toward the other for depriving us of needed support. That step requires only an event, remark, or circumstance that is perceived to mean that the Other is unconcerned about me, hostile toward me, annoyed with me. Note the emphasis is on perception. The actual intent is irrelevant. We behave and respond according to how we interpret others' behavior, not its actual meaning.

Selective Perception

Once mistrust of the Other's motives and feelings toward us begins, additional evidence gathers to corroborate our perception. Information accumulates to support pre-existing perceptions because of the distoring effect of "selective perception." We need the world around us to make sense—we need consistency. If new information doesn't fit with what we think we know, we distort the incoming information to make it consistent with the old. So new information passes through a perceptual filter that screeens out inconsistencies.

How does selective perception lead to interpersonal conflict? Because of our need for internal consistency, we distort our perceptions of interactions with others so that we selectively let in information that tells us "I am right." Information that tells us "I am wrong" does not pass so easily through our perceptual filters. So, bit by bit, data gather to form a convincing case that confirms our suspicions about the Other's feelings and attitudes about us.

Reality-Testing

Unless perceptions are tested against objective reality (what the Other really means), inaccuracies can grow. Talking together tests the accuracy of our perceptions against the replies of our partner. Effective day-to-day management of interpersonal differences requires conversation.

When interdependency is high and time for communication is limited, the burden on both persons' abilities to efficiently check out perceptions is heavy. Being busy people, time is seldom so abundant that the burden of reality-testing does not occasionally exceed our abilities to communicate, to hear and understand the Other.

The challenge posed by selective perception is daunting enough. But to make matters worse, we are simultaneously impaired by our two Wrong Reflexes—Non-communication and Power-play. These communication straight-jackets even further diminish our ability to stay in face-to-face contact long enough to complete the task of reaching an agreement.

Realistic Expectations

So it is that we face this stark situation in our everyday workplace relationships. How does the 4-Step Method help us? In the Dialogue, we:

■ remove the Wrong Reflexes by adopting the Cardinal Rules;

■ require sustained face-to-face discussion in the Essential Process; and

■ harness the power of several psychological forces toward harmony (to be discussed in Chapter 20).

As a result, we can expect to hear that the Other values our relationship, as do we (though not necessarily to an equal degree):

■ to learn about demands on the Other that prevent her being able to satisfy our needs;

■ to discover that some of our assumptions and perceptions about what he has been thinking and feeling are incorrect; and

■ to increase our mutual willingness to compromise in order to maintain the relationship.

But even these four modest outcomes must not be viewed as permanent gains that cannot be lost. Our struggle is like that of the frog attempting to escape from a well. He hops three inches, only to slide back two.

Relationships are not static. They are dynamic, living things that are buffeted daily by new events carried on the unrelenting tide of time. The improved mutual understanding and clarified perceptions resulting from Dialogue are covered by the sediment of each day's new events.

Figure 10:
A continuum of hope.

FANTASY	REALITY	ILLUSION
Wishful thinking		Despair
"No conflict should exist in a 'good' relationship."	"Conflict is inevitable, but differences can be managed."	"Situation is hopeless, differences are irreconcilable."

Maintenance

Interpersonal relationships need maintenance, just as machinery needs maintenance. Without regular attention to critical points in the system, deterioration in performance will result.

If a relationship has been painfully strained for a long time, one dose of this simple medicine may feel like dramatic progress. Its effects may last for days, weeks, or longer. For a more regularly maintained relationship, however, one dose may not have such dramatic effects, because harmony is not needed as desperately.

How do we maintain relationships? In productive, satisfying pairs, the Cardinal Rules are habitual, regular, even automatic. People talk to each other frequently. They do not resort to using the Wrong Reflexes, even under stress. They don't walk out on each other during arguments. They remain physically and emotionally accessible to the other while anger is expressed. They do not use coercion or intimidation to force the other to comply with their demands. Their decisions are made by mutual consent, not by one person overriding the Other's objections. And they acknowledge the Other's conciliatory gestures so that vulnerability, trust, and openness are rewarded rather than punished. These practices maintain good workplace relationships.

What Is a "Good" Relationship?

But, differences erupt into episodes of conflict in even the best of teams. Because people have needs that they properly expect the Other to satisfy, they are interdependent. Their needs, even when occasionally satisfied, do not disappear, just as hunger for food does not vanish forever just because you enjoy a satisfying meal.

So, the difference between a "good" interpersonal relationship in business and a "bad" one is not the presence or absence of conflict. The difference lies in the efficiency with which conflicts are resolved. Conflict is only resolved through communication. The 4-Step Method is designed specifically to aid communication in two-person relationships. Using this Method to resolve Clashes, and adopting the Cardinal Rules in routine communication, builds and maintains good, productive, satisfying relationships at work.

Chapter 17:

WHEN IT WORKS, WHEN IT WON'T

I herald bad news and good news. Bad news: The 4-Step Method does not work in all relationships. Good news: After you read this chapter, you will know when it works and when it won't.

The Clashes arising from differences in most relationships can be managed satisfactorily by this Method. Some conflicts, however, lack certain requirements necessary for success. This chapter describes the eight prerequisites to confidence that the 4-Step Method will work.

Personality Factors

When involved in "personality clashes," we often conclude that the conflict is irresolvable due to the Other's personality—the Bad-Person Illusion. In truth, certain personality factors can indeed impinge on the Method, making it less effective. So, some relevant personality factors will be mentioned as we list the eight prerequisites.

The 4-Step Method is designed for use when all of the following are true:

Prerequisite #1:
It Is a Two-Person Conflict

Some of the components of the Method are used in team building, interdepartmental problem solving, and labor contract negotiations, to name a few occasions where conflicts need resolution. However, when there are several conflicting parties, or when a party to the conflict consists of more than one person, a more complex resolution strategy is usually necessary.

Prerequisite #2:
The Two People Have an Ongoing, Interdependent Relationship

The participants must be in an important relationship that is not expected to end in the near future. You may be annoyed by the rudeness of a bank teller or the impatience of a telephone operator, but these relationships are not ongoing. Nor do you and he depend on each other for satisfaction of needs, except in very limited or infrequent transactions.

The 4-Step Method is normally inappropriate and unnecessary when a relationship exists only for the negotiation of one or a few issues, such as the purchase price of an item.

When there is no need to interact, there is no problem. Example: Employees whose jobs do not require that they work together. The individuals may not like each other, but their conflicts can best be managed by avoiding contact. Here, there is little consequence to using Wrong Reflex #1—Non-communication. Dislike between people who have no needs that the Other must satisfy is not an interpersonal conflict.

If a specific situation has come to mind while reading this section that you wish were resolved, but that does not seem to meet this prerequisite, then I suspect you are in fact interdependent. The needs you have of the Other may just be undefined.

Prerequisite #3:
Both People Are Present and Involved in the Dialogue

It takes two hands to clap. An interpersonal conflict is a dyadic, or two-person, process. One person can solve a personal problem; it takes two to solve an interpersonal problem. Without both parts of the dyad involved, the problem cannot be solved—the clapping makes no sound. The amount of interest each of you has in resolving the conflict may be unequal, and your levels of enthusiasm for talking about it may differ. If you question your Other's willingness to be involved, review the minimum requirements of your Other as discussed in Chapter 9. Surprisingly little commitment is expected of her to make the Method work.

Personality factor: *Schizoid Compromise*

Some people's experience in early childhood taught them that relationships are dangerous. They learned that being vulnerable to others carries a high risk of being hurt. Trusting brought abuse. Wanting love brought rejection.

The hurt that relationships can cause children is of two types: *invasion* (being emotionally suffocated, humiliated, battered) and *abandonment* (being neglected, left needy, unloved without emotional contact with others). Adults who suffered as children in these ways unconsciously keep emotionally distant from others as a protection against more hurt.

Of course, all of us keep a certain distance, fearing vulnerability, yet needing interpersonal contact. By the time we reach adulthood, we have usually found a comfortable compromise between emotional contact and withdrawal in our relationships. In psychotherapy, this comfort level is called the "schizoid compromise."

Due to having suffered painful invasion or abandonment as children, some people are unable to tolerate the anxiety aroused by sustained face-to-face contact with their Other, as required in the Dialogue. Being confronted with the Other's anger, and having the comfortingly familiar Wrong Reflexes outlawed by the Cardinal

Rules, can arouse intolerable fears. The primitive anxiety of being invaded and destroyed by the Other's anger, or of being abandoned and losing the relationship, can be too much to bear. Although Dialogues are tense encounters for everyone, some people find it impossible to remain engaged in uninterrupted issue-focused conversation. The more emotionally distant is one's schizoid compromise, the less able is the person to stay in the Essential Process, and therefore the effectiveness of the 4-Step Method is diminished.

Like other readers, you may think that this deeply psychological process does not apply to on-the-job relationships. It may seem to pertain only to intimate personal relationships, such as marriages. But psychological needs exist in workplaces too, along with task needs. And anxiety is aroused when we fear that these needs may not be met. The schizoid compromise is an anxiety-regulating mechanism that controls our behavior during conflicts in the workplace, just as it does in our personal lives.

Prerequisite #4:
Each Person Is Able to Refrain from Physical Violence

The Dialogue calls for participants to join in verbal, not physical, confrontation. Verbal aggression is permissible, and can even be helpful. Physical aggression, however, is neither. Not only is violent assault destructive to relationships, it is also illegal. Each person must be able to participate in discussion without fear that the Other's anger may erupt in physical attack.

Personality factor: *Impulsivity*

Most personality traits are present to some degree in all of us. "Impulsivity" is one such trait—the degree to which we have difficulty refraining from acting on our impulses. If your Other has a history of impulsive violence, then she may be unable to tolerate the stress of the Dialogue without violent outburst. You may not wish to risk provoking physical violence. Your personnel department or employee assistance program may be able to offer help.

Prerequisite #5:
Power Is Not Severely Imbalanced, and Neither Person Characteristically Abuses Power

Power is a characteristic of relationships, not of individuals. It is the capacity of one person to influence the behavior of the Other. This ability to influence the Other's behavior is related directly to the strength of the Other's needs. If Nguyen desperately needs Lucy's support, then Lucy is able to induce Nguyen to make concessions.

Power is nearly always a mutual process—each can affect the other. Hardly ever is one entirely powerless, although at times we may feel so because we fail to recognize our options.

The power in your relationship with your Other being mutual does not mean that it is balanced. The low-power partner (the one with the greatest needs of the Other) is most vulnerable in the Dialogue. Especially when power imbalance is great, your Other's promise to comply with Cardinal Rule #2 (Do not use Power-plays) is critically important. If you cannot trust the Other to accept this Cardinal Rule and not use the power at his disposal, then entering into a Dialogue might be risky.

Personality factor: *Sadism*

Some people derive pleasure from using power gratuitously to hurt others who are relatively helpless to respond. A pattern of such behavior is called sadism. Sadistic behavior is often associated with low self-esteem. Behaving sadistically produces a pleasurable feeling of power that compensates for their feelings of powerlessness and inadequacy.

For example, let's say you are in conflict with your boss and are wondering whether to suggest a meeting to talk it out. You know from past experience that she fires people for "making waves" or punishes "trouble-makers" by assigning undesirable tasks. She then likes to make a public display of the punishment around the office as an example to others. Your boss seems to enjoy wielding coercive, manipulative power. If you have no recourse to protect yourself from or deter her possible abuses, then using the 4-Step Method may not be prudent.

This example illustrates both power imbalance and sadistic abuse of power, as well as uncertain commitment to Cardinal Rule #2. If your Other has both the *ability* and *willingness* to coerce or intimidate you into submission to his demands, then using the 4-Step Method is risky. The Method requires that both people act according to the Cardinal Rules. Both participants must be willing to forego using coercive force, and to engage in the Dialogue as an alternative way of managing your differences.

Prerequisite #6:
Neither Person Is Addicted to a Chemical Substance

People who are alcoholic or dependent on other drugs suffer from a condition that jeopardizes the success of the 4-Step Method.

Certainly, a Dialogue should not be undertaken when either person is intoxicated or under the influence of drugs. But the dependency does not vanish just because the person is not intoxicated at the time. The dependency syndrome itself impairs the Method by disabling certain of the psychological forces toward harmony.

Personality factor: *Addictive Disorder*

People having the so-called "addictive personality" often hear an internal script telling them, "Nothing is ever enough." A desperate need to become satiated drives their compulsive consumption of the substance of their addiction. The problem this chronic hunger poses for the 4-Step Method is that an addictive Other will be difficult to satisfy with any amount of conciliation. The moment of Breakthrough will then be very difficult, perhaps impossible, to reach. The addicted person (who is not recovering or in treatment) may complicate the process by employing the "covering up" behavior habitually used in hiding the addiction from associates.

Prerequisite #7:
Neither Person Suffers from Severe Emotional Disturbance

"Emotional disturbance" is a loose collection of personality factors that impinge on the effectiveness of the 4-Step Method. In particular, people who are acutely *paranoid* (a neurosis or psychosis) or *sociopathic* (a character disorder) have distorted perceptions of their relationships that make the Method a poor risk.

All of us employ defenses against anxiety that distort our perceptions of social reality. So even normal, well-adjusted people may occasionally exhibit behavioral symptoms similar to paranoia or sociopathy. These normal ego-defenses are especially likely during periods of high stress.

But this so-called "normal neurosis" does not disable the 4-Step Method. Most people who have emotional problems severe enough to render the Dialogue ineffective have some history of psychiatric hospitalization or closely supervised outpatient treatment. Our personality quirks and maladjustments are most apparent to the people closest to us. Just because your Other may sometimes seem "crazy" does not mean the Method will not work.

You may consider yourself unqualified to assess whether these emotional disturbances are present in your Other. Even if you are in doubt, you can probably try the 4-Step Method without great risk. If it doesn't work for these reasons, damage is not likely. Your Dialogue will simply be another unfulfilling argument that may not seem unlike many previous encounters.

Prerequisite #8:
Both People Speak the Same Language

Rarely could two people have an ongoing interdependent relationship in the workplace who do not regularly communicate in a common language. However, if Clashes between people who cannot communicate verbally were to arise, the 4-Step Method would be difficult to carry out. After all, the Dialogue does entail face-to-face communication.

All of the Above

After reading this chapter, you may be thinking, "All of my conflicts are with sociopathic, sadistic, paranoid drug addicts who have me under their thumb." If such a thought discourages you from using the 4-Step Method in a relationship that matters to you, refresh your understanding of the Bad-Person Illusion in Chapter 4.

PART 4

Chapter 18:

INTRODUCTION TO THE BEHAVIORAL SCIENCE OF DIFFERENCE-MANAGEMENT

As discussed in Chapter 3, the 4-Step Method is a behavioral prescription. Follow the prescription, and reap the results. It works, even if you don't know the theory that explains why it works.

So why is a section about behavioral science included in this book? Some readers are mediators, consultants, students, and academicians who have a professional interest in theories of difference-management. Other readers just enjoy learning new ways of understanding their own behavior.

If you have no professional or academic interest in this field, but simply would like practical guidance in building better relationships at work, you might choose not to read the remaining chapters. Just use the 4-Step Method as it has already been presented. But those of you whose interest extends beyond a personal one will find Part 4 of the book of special benefit.

Mental Maps

Each one of us has, whether or not we are aware of it, a "mental map" that guides our behavior throughout each day. A mental map is a system of beliefs and assumptions that provides a sense of orderliness and predictability in our personal worlds. Our mental maps provide the basis of the hundreds of automatic decisions about how to act that we make each day. Your mental map differs from mine because our past experiences have been different, giving us different assumptions about how to behave in the world in order to get what we want from it.

When we are interacting with others, we are behaving. We are acting and reacting, talking and responding. Our behavior is not random. It is ordered and purposeful to the extent that our mental maps guide our behavior. We assume, whether correctly or not, that acting in a particular way will produce an intended outcome. If I am yelling at you, it is because I assume that "Impressing on you the strength of my anger will cause you to give in to me." If I walk out and slam the door, my mental map has led me to believe that "Showing you how hurt I am will make you feel sorry for me, and then you will let me have my way" or perhaps "Conflicts are hopeless; it's best to avoid them."

These internal scripts come from past experiences that taught us lessons. Each of these old lessons (many of which may not have come from good teachers) provided information that today make up parts of our mental maps about how to manage interpersonal differences.

This information establishes a causal ("if-then") link between behavioral options and the likely consequences of each option. Since we generally attempt to behave in ways that will promote our own self-interests, these if-then links constitute a chain of assumptions that guide our way toward desired outcomes.

Figure 11:
Mental maps.

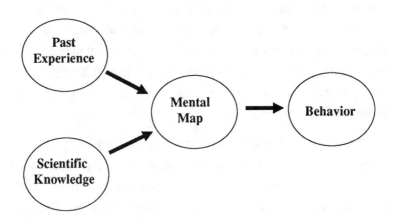

Revising Our Mental Maps

Scientifically sound theories, models, and concepts supply accurate information about how to behave when in conflict that can help us revise parts of our mental maps so that they serve as more reliable guides to where we want to go—satisfying, productive, harmonious relationships. For example, the part of my map that says "Walking out will make you feel sorry for me" might change to "Walking out will only deepen your resentment toward me and make it harder to resolve this." This changed if-then link in my map will cause me to act differently in future conflicts.

This chapter introduces the behavioral science of difference-management. The concepts and models that follow come to us from several disciplines—particularly psychology, sociology, communication theory, organizational behavior, cultural anthropology, and ethology. I have made no attempt to be comprehensive in reviewing relevant scientific literature, nor to report research from original sources. Rather, I have synthesized information from several fields that helps us understand the anatomy of interpersonal differences and how they can be managed constructively. Although most of this information is accepted scientific theory, some ideas are somewhat controversial. Certain parts are my own informed speculation that I hope the reader will regard as worthy of consideration. Whether they be proven facts or the subjects of informed debate, the ideas presented here will add more detail to your mental map.

Chapter 19:

DYNAMICS OF INTERPERSONAL CONFLICT

Interpersonal conflict is a system of behavior. Like other complex systems, it is comprised of many interrelated subsystems that contain elements which interact dynamically. In this chapter, we will look at four relevant dynamics of interpersonal conflict:

- Issues in conflict
- The retaliatory cycle
- Confrontation and conciliation phases
- The ambivalence-projection-polarization chain

ISSUES IN CONFLICT

"Issues" may be thought of as "matters of concern" to participants. In every conflict, there are three kinds of issues that concern the parties: substantive, emotional, and pseudo-substantive.

Substantive Issues

Unless you and your Other have jointly adopted a policy of Non-communication to cope with your differences, you have arguments. Your arguments are about issues, the matters of mutual concern. You may argue with a co-worker about whose turn it is to answer the phones, or with your boss about whether your performance review was properly conducted, or with your sales manager about whether you are capable of handling important customers. The subjects of these arguments are "substantive issues." Taken at face value, substantive issues are matters that concern the participants and therefore are the problem to be solved or the question to be decided.

Positions

Each person holds a position on the disputed substantive issue that differs from the position held by the Other. You think that since you have an urgent project to complete, your co-worker should answer the phones; he thinks that, since his job description does not include answering phones, he should not be required to do it. You think your job performance merits a satisfactory rating; your boss insists that it calls for an unsatisfactory evaluation. You want to be given full responsibility for a key customer; your sales manager thinks that you have not yet developed the skills to handle such a large account. Your statements during the argument are attempts to persuade the Other to accept your position, and vice versa.

At this time, let me introduce you to Susan, an unnoticed observer of these arguments. Susan assumes that resolving a conflict is simply a matter of finding a mutually acceptable compromise position on the substantive issues being argued, or possibly finding some previously unrecognized alternative position that satisfies both participants' self-interests. Be forewarned: Susan is in for an education in the next few pages.

Emotional Issues

After some reflection on what she witnessed during your latest argument, Susan notices that the conflict was not simply a difference of opinion—a reasonable, unemotional discussion. An unemotional difference of opinion is distinctly different from a tense or angry encounter. The latter is what we call a "conflict." A mere difference of opinion is seldom regarded as a problem—just a subject for conversation. The angry argument she observed was clearly not just a conversation.

Noticing this distinction helps Susan to recognize that when people are in conflict, emotional matters of concern must also be involved—what we will call "emotional issues."

Personal Needs and Emotional Issues

What might be the emotional issues in a conflict between co-workers about answering phones, or between you and your boss about the accuracy of your performance appraisal, or between you and your sales manager about handling important customers? Emotional issues fall into a rather small number of categories:

1) Issues of POWER, deriving from individual needs for control and influence over others, and for the social status created by power differences.

2) Issues of APPROVAL, deriving from individual needs for affection—to be liked.

3) Issues of INCLUSION, deriving from individual needs for acceptance into social groups.

4) Issues of JUSTICE, deriving from individual needs to be treated fairly, equally, and equitably.

5) Issues of IDENTITY, deriving from individual needs for autonomy, self-esteem, positive self-image, self-determination, and affirmation of personal values.

Whether these categories are exhaustive or mutually exclusive is unimportant. Our point here is that emotional issues underlie arguments about substantive issues. In fact, the presence of emotional issues is what distinguishes a "conflict" from a "disagreement." That is, disputed issues not only impact objective self-interest—they are also felt to be important to the extent that they are vehicles for the resolution of emotional issues.

To Know Thyself

Emotional issues are not as easy to recognize as substantive issues. In the heat of argumentative battle, we generally do not mention them. In the workplace, we don't often speak of our needs for power, our needs to be liked and approved of, or our needs to be socially included. For better or worse, social and organizational norms typically discourage open disclosure of these needs. After years of learning how to fit in, we have incorporated these norms so deeply that we are often not even consciously aware of our own emotional issues. Being unaware of them, we have difficulty "getting in touch" with how we feel and describing these feelings clearly.

Even so, these fundamental human needs are present in each of us. So, in every interpersonal dispute, emotional issues supply the energy that fuels the flames of conflict. They are the fire in us that our foes try to douse with logical persuasion.

Unbeknownst to the douser, however, our persuasive efforts to put out the fire are often the emotional equivalent of gasoline. Attempting to change the Other's mind with facts and logic only increases his conviction that he is right. His personal needs that spawn emotional issues cannot be reduced or satisfied through persuasion, argument, or logical reasoning. On the contrary, we cling ever more dearly to our positions as the Other refuses to recognize the superior logic of our position. His stubborn resistance to accepting our position on the substantive issue only lends further evidence to our belief that he is wrong. The heat of battle intensifies.

Remember Susan, our scientifically curious observer? She can now identify the substantive and emotional issues in the conflicts she witnessed a while ago. She recognizes that each co-worker who does not want to answer phones needs to have control over the solution (an issue of power). She recognizes that the employee's need to feel fairly evaluated is violated by the boss's review of his performance (an issue of justice). She recognizes that the salesperson who seeks the challenge of handling important clients needs to affirm her self-esteem as a competent professional (an issue of identity).

We might conclude that conflict resolution is achieved by bringing emotional issues out of the protective darkness of silence, and into the light of open discussion. Not so fast, Susan cautions. There is more to understand.

With ever-increasing insight, Susan notices that disputants often become reconciled, resolved, conciliatory, and more trusting without having come to a specific agreement on the substantive issue they were arguing about. But even more surprisingly, the emotional needs underlying the substantive issues may not have been directly addressed and resolved. This is puzzling. If not by a reasoned exchange of views on the contested issues, how do conflicts become resolved?

Pseudo-substantive Issues

Susan has noticed a curious phenomenon that may provide a clue to the answer. She observes that during arguments, additional issues are brought up and disputed. The contesters then stake out opposing positions on these new issues and treat them as though they are substantive. Often, these additional, apparently substantive issues had not been mentioned previously. Sometimes, they are awakened from a hibernation that began in a previous season of the disputants' relationship.

Susan has also noticed that, when reconciliation eventually does occur, many of these new subjects of argument are ignored—no agreement is reached on them. How can this happen? Were these substantive issues actually unimportant? Is reconciling different positions on substantive issues actually unnecessary? If so, what was the argument really about? Susan begins to suspect that the process of solving conflicts is not as logical as she had first assumed.

A Deception of Self and Other

Susan's suspicions are correct. The "substantive" issues being argued were not as substantive as they appeared at face value. Having one's preferred position accepted by the Other was not all that mattered—perhaps this was not even a significant concern. The apparently substantive issues were, to some degree, "pseudo-substantive." That is, they were partially or even wholly false, not materially related to the disputants' objective underlying interests. But why are pseudo-substantive issues present in conflicts? What purpose do they serve?

Issues are substantive to the extent that they represent objective, rational underlying self-interests. Issues are pseudo-substantive to the extent that they serve to satisfy individual needs related to emotional issues. So, any disputed issue can be, and usually is, both substantive and pseudo-substantive.

To summarize how the three kinds of issues are related: **Pseudo-substantive** issues are **emotional** issues disguised as **substantive** issues.

Susan is dismayed. How can two people in conflict ever sort out rational self-interest from unconsciously generated pseudo-substantive issues? Fortunately, recalling Chapter 15, Susan recognizes that resolution is not rational—"The problem does not have to be solved for the conflict to be resolved." The remainder of Part 4 will guide Susan's rational mind through this paradox.

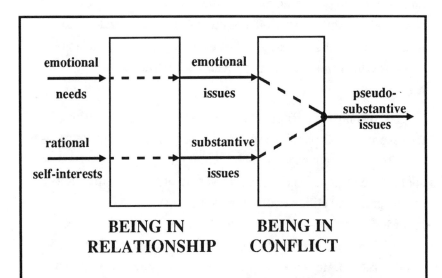

Figure 12:
Substantive, Emotional, and Pseudo-substantive issues.

emotional
needs

rational
self-interests

emotional
issues

substantive
issues

pseudo-
substantive
issues

**BEING IN
RELATIONSHIP**

**BEING IN
CONFLICT**

Explanation: Emotional needs and rational self-interests are individual concerns; emotional issues and substantive issues are relationship concerns. Individual concerns become relationship concerns when we interact with others. Conflict causes emotional and substantive issues to fuse, becoming pseudo-substantive issues.

Illustration

Let's consider the case of Brad who disputes his most recent performance evaluation by his boss, Jeanine. Brad's somewhat negative evaluation is of substantive concern to him to the extent that his salary and career progress may be affected. It is pseudo-substantive to the extent that it affects his self-esteem, status among co-workers, and feelings of being treated fairly. In the proportion that it affects both, the issue is both substantive and pseudo-substantive.

But this is not the first time that Brad has felt he was treated unfairly by his boss. Previous instances of perceived unfair treatment produced feelings of resentment but the issues were never discussed with Jeanine. These old resentments have accumulated to form a pool of "angry energy." The negative performance evaluation raises the level of the pool to overflowing. He shouts angrily at her.

The display of anger directed at Jeanine is not in proportion to the severity of this particular insult—the somewhat negative evaluation. Brad's pent-up anger requires venting far beyond what is an appropriate response to the present issue. In order to dissipate left-over anger, Brad criticizes other areas that are not related to the immediate problem—her sketchy technical knowledge, outdated style of dress, and overall incompetency as a manager (pseudo-substantive issues). He is discharging anger from the reservoir within.

Some of these pseudo-substantive issues have some actual impact on Brad's self-interest; others are entirely irrelevant. But he himself is unaware of this. He is deceiving himself into believing that the pseudo-substantive issues are actually substantive. The conflict between Brad and Jeanine compounds as Brad expresses these criticisms of Jeanine to other employees, creating tension and contaminating others' relationships with her.

The self-deception inherent in pseudo-substantive issues is unconscious and reflexive, not premeditated or consciously intended. Although past experience has shaped how we do it, the psychological mechanism that creates pseudo-substantive issues is inherited. It is a psycho-biological process that we are born with and will have until we die, and will genetically pass on to our children. It is human nature. By learning new skills and gaining new insights into behavior we can manage our behavior more constructively, but we cannot eliminate the process within us that creates pseudo-substantive issues.

Implications

How does our understanding of the three kinds of issues guide us in managing interpersonal differences?

- Managing differences does not necessarily require agreement to be reached on any particular substantive issue. Disputed issues may be largely pseudo- substantive, having little impact on objective underlying self-interests. To that degree, compromises and concessions may be easily exchanged between participants.

- Conflict resolution requires the discharge of angry energy accumulated from previous frustration.

- Participants in conflict cannot be expected to act reasonably or logically until angry energy has been discharged.

THE RETALIATORY CYCLE

Periodically an event triggers conflict which evidences itself through an exchange of hostile behaviors. We commonly refer to this exchange as a "fight."

For example, the triggering event may be a request by a colleague to answer the phone while she is at lunch. This seemingly innocent request launches the co-workers into another fight about whose responsibility it is to answer phones. As the argument continues, accusations, self-defensive explanations, attacks, and counterattacks are exchanged. The pair is engaged in a "retaliatory cycle."

Figure 13:
The Retaliatory Cycle.

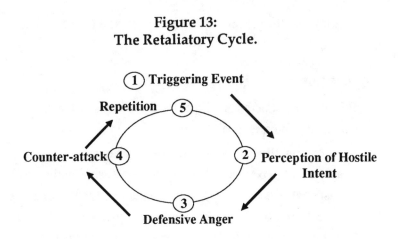

The sequence of events in the retaliatory cycle are as follows:

1) *Triggering event.* Any verbal or non-verbal behavior by Person A.

2) *Perception of hostile intent.* Person B perceives that he is the target of hostile motives, as manifested by the triggering event.

3) *Defensive anger.* The natural and automatic emotional response to perceiving that one is being attacked.

4) *Counterattack.* Person B's defensive anger is transformed into an aggressive response directed toward Person A, intended as a self-protective measure.

5) *Repetition.* Person B's counterattack may be perceived by Person A as an unprovoked triggering event. This sequence then becomes an endless loop from which there is no natural escape. Each participant feels unable to safely stop the cycle without accepting defeat.

This is the anatomy of a fight.

Working in highly social organizations, we can and usually do exercise self-control in preventing the retaliatory cycle from escalating to violence. There are, of course, tragic occasions where participants' self-control has been inadequate. Still, the retaliatory cycle is psychologically primitive in origin, and is biologically rooted in our ancient past. The reflexes are powerful and are not fully controlled by willpower. The retaliatory cycle is a typical, even universal, form of interaction during interpersonal conflicts.

Implications

How does understanding the mechanics of the retaliatory cycle help us manage differences? During the Dialogue of the 4-Step Method,

■ It is helpful if perceptions are tested for accuracy by describing one's assumptions about the Other's motives. This reality-testing can lead to discovery that a triggering event was not motivated by hostility.

■ Acceptance of Cardinal Rule #1 (*Do not withdraw*) is necessary to prevent withdrawal from communication. The Wrong Reflex of Non-communication is often experienced by others as a hostile tactic. Mutual Non-communication is an "armed standoff" that deprives each participant of satisfaction of needs. This uneasy truce only temporarily suspends the retaliatory cycle; it does not stop the fight. Cardinal Rule #1 reinstates communication, the lifeblood of resolution.

■ Acceptance of Cardinal Rule #2 (*Do not use Power-play*) is necessary to prevent the use of coercive force or intimidation from causing the conflict to escalate toward violence. Force begets force. Each increase in the level of force brings a corresponding increase in retaliation by the Other. With each escalating round of the cycle, the stakes are raised for each participant, making it ever more difficult to find a face-saving way to escape from the cycle.

CONFRONTATION AND CONCILIATION PHASES

Most of us can recall a "good fight" with a spouse that somehow led to renewed intimacy, or a "frank discussion" with a colleague that resulted in regained trust and cooperation, or a "heart-to-heart talk" with an offended friend that brought the return of warmth and mutual support.

We can also recall many episodes of the retaliatory cycle that left us upset and angry. On such occasions, a reservoir of angry energy remained within us, tugging at our self-restraint, demanding an outlet.

What accounts for the difference between these two experiences? Why do fights sometimes lead to resolution, and at other times bring only frustration? Often, the difference is whether the fight was permitted to continue through completion of the "confrontation" phase and proceed to the "conciliation" phase of the encounter.

Hydraulic Theory of Emotion

Eons of interpersonal conflict have contributed popular expressions to modern language that describe this experience: "letting off steam," "getting things off your chest," "blowing your top." These phrases suggest a "hydraulic theory" of emotion, indicating that pressure contained within a closed system seeks release through some outlet.

The validity of the hydraulic theory of emotion is debated among behavioral scientists. Whether or not you subscribe to the theory, the indisputable fact is that time for confrontation within an appropriate context normally precedes emotional readiness to reconcile. An analogy of the confrontation and conciliation phases is presented as the "Conflict Mountain":

Figure 14:
The "Conflict Mountain": Confrontation and conciliation phases.

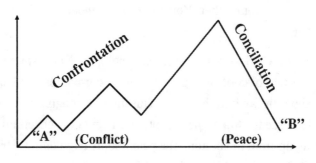

Join me in plotting a journey. Imagine that you are at point "A" and wish to travel to point "B." Between you and your destination stands a mountain. No road bypasses the mountain, so you must travel up to the peak, then down. So it is impossible to get to "B" without enduring the difficult part of the journey, the upward climb. Nor is it possible to go down before going up. "A" precedes "B." This is an inescapable fact, like it or not.

Point "A" represents a state of unresolved conflict with your Other. You wish that your relationship were harmonious and effective, rather than tense and unproductive. These objectives lie at

---

your destination, point "B." The "conflict mountain" stands between you and your goal. The stressful upward journey that you must travel first is the confrontation phase; the more pleasant downward part is the conciliation phase.

You wish that you could magically find yourself in agreement with your Other. But magic is not of the natural world. Human nature (psychology) is a part of the world, just as is "mountain nature" (geology). The height of the mountain symbolizes the amount of escalation necessary before one can proceed to reconciliation. You may have to scale the mountain to intimidating heights. Also, it is not a journey you can travel alone, at your own pace; you can only go there with your Other. You are interdependent, as if handcuffed together.

Often, when we find ourselves at point "A" and aspire to point "B," our fear of confronting the Other is so great that we hardly get started before we quit the climb. Our dread is magnified by being unable to see the top of the mountain. Its height is uncertain, but looking up from the bottom, the peak looms frighteningly high. We believe that danger lurks at high altitudes and that we, as individuals or as a relationship, might be hurt if we climb too high.

Another apprehension about starting to climb together is that past experiences have revealed the Other's habit is quitting part way up, leaving us up there all alone. So, we often take the safe option of not starting the climb at all.

But climbing the mountain is the *only* way to get to point "B." We sometimes try to act as if we are already at point "B," doing our best to act polite. But triggering events remind us that we really are not there yet. So, we wait beside the mountain, making false starts from time to time, feeling helplessly dependent on the other to show signs of trustworthiness, or hoping that some magical vehicle will transport us effortlessly to point "B."

Implications

The existence of confrontation and conciliation phases of the Dialogue means that:

- It is necessary to engage in confrontation before we can expect resolution and harmony.

- It is necessary to ensure that neither person will abandon the journey before reaching point "B."

- The risk of harm to the relationship from escalation is real, but is perceptually exaggerated. It may be helpful to set some groundrules for the Dialogue that will prevent the escalation from being greater than necessary.

AMBIVALENCE, PROJECTION, AND POLARIZATION

Because the world is not simple, we are ambivalent about most things. That is, we have few feelings, needs, or wishes that are not in conflict with opposing feelings, needs, and wishes. We may like our jobs, but we also find our jobs frustrating and stressful. We may respect our boss, but also find him annoying and sometimes offensive.

Few wishes or needs are so simple that we are not ambivalent about them. Certainly our feelings toward the significant Others in our lives are not uniformly positive. We feel both attraction and repulsion, like and dislike, respect and disrespect.

Cognitive Dissonance

Having two incompatible experiences at the same time is inherently uncomfortable. Psychologists call this discomfort "cognitive dissonance." We strive to reduce dissonance and replace it with consonance.

For example, Patricia considers herself a shrewd and conservative investor, yet she recently lost $10,000 on a speculative stock. The two experiences, "I am a shrewd investor" and "I bought a loser," are incompatible. Patricia attempts to regain cognitive consonance by adjusting her perceptions so that the two experiences are no longer in conflict. In this case, she might tell herself that "It wasn't my fault that a hurricane wiped out the company's headquarters in Puerto Rico." This rationalization permits Patricia to retain her self-concept as a wise investor in the face of evidence that she took a bath in the stock market. These attitude adjustments almost always take place unconsciously and automatically.

Ambivalence, as it occurs in conflict, produces cognitive dissonance. When we are ambivalent about a particular substantive issue, we are not entirely "of one mind." We may not be absolutely certain what to believe, or which position to support on a complex issue. Perceiving correctness in two alternative positions, both of which cannot be correct, is inherently incompatible and discomforting.

To illustrate these dynamics, let's sit in on a project team meeting at the Hard Core Manufacturing Company. The team is discussing two options: (1) to delay production of a new widget in order to ensure quality, or (2) to meet the deadline in spite of likely quality problems. Each of these two positions has both merits and drawbacks.

Projection

As a member of the team, Erin is unsure which position to espouse. Her uneasy ambivalence seeks resolution. Here, dissonance is the anxiety aroused by Erin's awareness of not knowing an answer and, at the same time, thinking of herself as a smart person. The ego-defense mechanism of "projection" provides a way for Erin to reduce the tension of cognitive dissonance caused by ambivalence and achieve consonance.

When we "project," we attribute some undesired characteristic of ourselves to another person. That is, we see it in the Other rather than in ourselves. By projecting this characteristic onto the Other, it is eliminated from ourselves, and so our dissonance is reduced.

Projecting to Reduce Ambivalence

Projection is a mechanism for lowering the ambivalence that arouses dissonance. By attributing one side of our ambivalence about some issue onto another person, we can then perceive the Other as supporting a belief or position that we reject.

Let's say that to reduce her ambivalence about the issue before her team, Erin chooses to espouse position #1, to delay production. Once her choice is made, Erin feels relieved of ambivalence by achieving resolution on the issue.

How do we decide which side of our ambivalence to support and which side to project, if not on the merits of the two positions? Erin's choice to support position #1 is somewhat arbitrary because the data are incomplete that would conclusively prove which option is better. Significant decisions are always made under conditions of uncertainty—otherwise they would be easy and we would all agree. But once the choice is made, or human egos demand that "that which is me" is favored over "that which is not me." Once projected, the denied part of herself—the "not me" part—becomes inherently negative, undesirable. Erin's adaptive mind then goes to work unconsciously rearranging her analysis of information about the issue so that she views the rejected position (to not delay) as a bad idea. A decision has been made, although it may not be the best decision.

From *Intra*personal to *Inter*personal Conflict

This mental maneuvering removes Erin's ambivalence and thereby reduces her cognitive dissonance. That is, it resolves her intrapersonal conflict—the conflict within herself. But reducing ambivalence through projection has a troubling side effect: It creates interpersonal conflict.

Erin's intrapsychic harmony, won by this self-manipulation, is short-lived. A few moments later in the team meeting, her colleague, Mark, while exploring pros and cons of the two options, points out a merit of position #2, that production should not be delayed. In making this comment, Mark unwittingly threatens Erin's new-found intrapsychic harmony—being "of one mind"—and presents himself as a convenient target for her projection. Giving Mark's comment serious consideration would rekindle her ambivalence, so she is obliged to perceive it as an unworthy idea.

Mark may or may not have reached a decision on the issue—he simply pointed out a bit of data. But Erin has projected onto him the belief that production should not be delayed. She had rejected that position in order to reduce the intrapsychic tension of ambivalence; it is now an unwanted, denied, former part of herself. So she now perceives that Mark holds that belief, rather than herself. Now, instead of struggling with her internal indecision, Erin can act out the struggle interpersonally. We see the beginning of a two-person conflict.

Regarding herself as a good problem solver, Erin must now protect that part of her self-concept by ensuring that other team members agree with her. As the team's discussion continues, she points out the flaws in Mark's position. Since the issue of whether to delay is a complex and controversial one, she can use very reasonable and sound arguments in doing so. If Erin can persuade others that she is correct, then she must surely have made the right choice. She convinces herself by convincing others.

Personalization

Like us all, Erin must maintain a positive self-concept. This requires that she believe her position is correct. It also leads to her opinion that Mark's holding an opposite position must mean that he is not only incorrect but also defective in some way. Why else would someone believe something opposite to her belief? Regardless of past assurances that "reasonable people may disagree," our natural ego-defense requirements urge us to assume that people who believe differently from us must be flawed.

So, in order to maintain her cognitive consonance, Erin questions Mark's competency. He obviously must be uninformed or prejudiced, as demonstrated by his support of a wrong idea. Further ego-protection is achieved by believing that anyone who supports that idea is not only wrong, but is also stupid. Erin has now "personalized" the conflict; that is, she has attributed the reason for their conflict to the personal characteristics of her Other, Mark.

In projecting and personalizing the conflict it is Erin's own anxieties about being incompetent, uninformed, prejudiced, and stupid that are relieved by seeing those flaws in Mark.

Meanwhile back in the team meeting, Mark, being only human, is simultaneously going through the same ambivalence-reduction process across the table from her. His conclusion is that meeting the deadline is the correct solution to the team's problem, and that anyone who thinks otherwise must be stupid. This is the anatomy of a "personality conflict."

Polarization

This mutual projection of rejected positions on substantive issues reduces intrapsychic ambivalence for both Mark and Erin. But it also leads to polarization. That is, each has projected onto the other the unwanted side of their intrapersonal ambivalence on the issue, and are now arguing about it. Erin's original *intra*personal conflict is now being acted out as an *inter*personal conflict. Since egos cannot permit letting in disconfirming information that would arouse ambivalence, each person must introduce new data to support the correctness of their preferred positions on the "substantive" issue—largely pseudo-substantive, since it serves as a vehicle for meeting emotional needs. Erin and Mark have polarized to the extent that they seem to hold totally opposite positions on the issue of whether to meet the production deadline. Agreement now seems increasingly difficult to achieve unless one gives in to the other and accepts defeat. They have created a win-lose conflict.

This ambivalence-projection-polarization chain helps explain the puzzling phenomenon that people who are closest to each other fight the most. Employees wonder why they ever took a job in an organization full of such crazy, incompetent people. Married couples constantly fight, leading to the conclusion that they have such opposite personalities, such "irreconcilable differences," that divorce is the only answer.

Figure 15:
The ambivalence-projection-polarization chain.

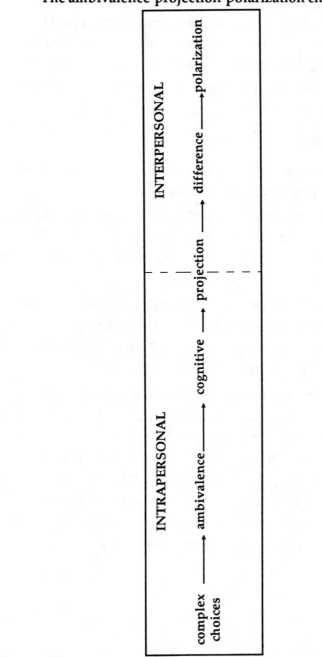

A gloomy picture? No hope for compatibility? The fact that we sustain long-term, interdependent relationships is testimony to a remarkable ability. Tolerating ambivalence, and refraining from premature projection onto others to defend our egos against the anxiety aroused by intrapsychic ambivalence, is no easy task. Still, especially under stressful conditions, this destructive sequence of events is all too common.

Implications

How does understanding the ambivalence-projection- polarization model help us manage our differences?

- A lengthy period of face-to-face talking may be needed to get each participant's actual positions communicated, to "reality test" projections, leading to recognition that they are inaccurate.

- Conciliatory gestures help to resolve so-called "personality conflicts" by eroding the destructive tendencies to find fault with the Other (personalize) and exaggerate differences between oneself and the Other (polarize).

- Participants' understandable and natural needs to maintain positive self-concepts (defense of ego) must be met in ways that do not increase interpersonal conflict. Projection of negative attributes to the Other, which is the typical device for meeting ego-support needs in conflict situations, must be reduced. A both-gain or fair compromise solution to substantive issues must be found, effectively reducing the need to protect the ego from assault.

On to Harmony

This chapter has described several behavioral and mental events that occur during episodes of human conflict. Each of the models contains several elements that interact dynamically. With our understanding of these dynamics, we will next explore the forces that are present in two-person conflicts which the 4-Step Method harnesses to transform conflict into harmony.

Chapter 20:

FORCES TOWARD HARMONY

Happily, all the psychological dynamics at play in two-person relationships do not promote conflict. Others work in the opposite direction, helping turn conflict into cooperation and tension into harmony.

Once the retaliatory cycle has begun, a key event must happen for resolution of conflict to occur: One of the participants must offer a conciliatory gesture. Someone must indicate a willingness to agree, to compromise, to stop fighting. Without such a gesture, mutual retaliation would continue indefinitely. So before examining the psychological forces toward harmony, let's first sharpen our understanding of the intriguing phenomenon of conciliatory gestures. Then we will look at four forces harnessed by the 4-Step Method that cause them to happen.

CONCILIATORY GESTURES

Everyone knows from personal experience that not all conflicts are chronic, endless, interpersonal tragedies. Many episodes of the retaliatory cycle result in agreement and renewed trust. How does this transformation take place? The simplest answer is: Conflicts end because conciliatory gestures happen.

What is a conciliatory gesture? As discussed briefly in Chapter 11, it is a behavior that indicates a shift in attitude from me-against-you to us-against-the-problem. The gesture is usually a verbal statement or question, but can be a non-verbal expression of the same message. It reveals a desire or openness to resolve the conflict in a mutually acceptable way. The element common to all conciliatory gestures is that expressing them makes one vulnerable to the Other. It presents an opportunity for the Other to score a point in the win-lose game.

Forms of conciliatory gestures:

- Apologizing

- Expressing regret for one's past behavior

- Conceding on a contested issue

- Offering to compromise

- Expressing empathy for the Other's problems

- Recognizing the legitimacy of the Other's point of view

- Revealing one's own underlying needs and emotional issues

- Disclosing one's thoughts, feelings, motives, and past history as they pertain to the conflict

- Asking for honest feedback

- Expressing positive feelings for the Other, such as affection, admiration, respect

- Accepting personal responsibility for part of the problem

- Initiating search for both-gain solutions

Conciliatory gestures often go unnoticed, even by the one who made the gesture. They are skittish creatures that dart cautiously through the shadowy underbrush of the verbal forest. Sometimes they appear as double-entendres whose intended meaning is ambiguous.

Often, due to personality or situational factors, one person is more forthcoming with these gestures than is the Other. But in effectively managed conflict, there eventually is an exchange of conciliatory gestures that promptly results in relaxation of tension. When this welcome moment arrives, the sigh of relief is sometimes audible.

This vital exchange is the Breakthrough part of the 4-Step Method. The Breakthrough introduces an improved emotional climate that opens a window of opportunity for participants to make a Deal about changes in each one's future behavior that will accommodate the concerns of the Other.

FOUR FORCES

The Breakthrough is the product of several psychological forces harnessed by the Method that act in concert to turn conflict into cooperation, interpersonal war into interpersonal peace. Although other constructive forces may also contribute, this chapter will focus on those that seem most powerful:

- **Fatigue**
- **Desire for peace**
- **Catharsis**
- **Inhibitory reflex**

Let's explore each of these forces in turn, starting with the most obvious and concrete and moving toward the more obscure and psychodynamic.

Fatigue

People get tired of fighting. Fighting is hard work. We "wear down" and want to stop, to end an unpleasant encounter. Once we see that we cannot "win" the conflict by persuading the Other to accept our demands, we may then see agreeing as the only remaining alternative to continued fighting.

Although it is the most obvious factor, fatigue alone is not sufficient to bring genuine reconciliation. If it were the only influence toward agreement, then conciliatory gestures would have a shallow tone, sounding like, "Okay, okay, have it your way. Let's agree to something so we can get out of here." Agreements resting only on this foundation would be short-lived at best. But, in combination with the more optimistic forces to follow, fatigue can trigger a participant's willingness to move toward agreement.

Desire for Peace

Being in conflict is inherently unpleasant. Still, many of us perversely seem to like something about it. We all know people who "pick fights" with others for no apparent reason. Let's take a moment to examine this perversity before describing the desire for peace as a force toward harmony.

Early Learning

We learned much as children. Developmental psychologists estimate that our social behavior is mostly determined before we become teenagers, possibly much younger. If our early family environment was characterized by much fighting and arguing, then we learned that conflict is how people engage with other people. Conflict then becomes comfortingly familiar—"better the devil we know than the one we don't." As adults, we reproduce that familiar pattern of social interaction in our own families and workplaces.

Displaced Aggression

Another factor stirs up conflict, causing it to burst spontaneously into flames without evident reason. All of us, for periods of time, experience chronic frustration, feeling deprived of satisfactions we believe we are entitled to. Feeling unfairly deprived produces "floating anger" or irritability that lies hidden under the surface of shared waters like a mine awaiting a passing ship. When the mine is inad-

vertently struck by a co-worker or boss, it explodes. Tl
is called displaced aggression.

If this mine-laying were conscious or intentional,
cuse the perpetrator of engaging in interpersonal terrorism. But,
since it is unwitting, it is more forgivable. The terrorist, also hurt in
the blast, is a victim as well. Still, the innocent victim who happens
to be in the wrong place at the wrong time will indignantly protest,
"What did I do to deserve this?"

Illustration

A tongue-in-cheek illustration of displaced aggression goes like
this:

Kristie is criticized by her boss at work one day. Respecting her
superiors, she dutifully accepts the criticism without retort. Coming
home frustrated after work that night, Kristie yells at her spouse,
Dale, for not buying groceries on the way home from his day at the
office. Dale, hoping to maintain marital harmony, stifles his annoyance and instead spanks their child, Junior, for some minor
infraction. Junior, being a well-behaved child, does not retort, but
instead kicks the dog, Spot. Spot, being an obedient dog, rather than
biting Junior, chases the cat, Kitty. Kitty, recognizing the futility of
fighting Spot, kills a mouse. So the mouse pays the ultimate price
for Kristie's boss criticizing her at work that day.

So, the comfortable familiarity of learned behavior patterns,
combined with misdirected aggression arising from floating anger,
propel us into episodes of conflict that can seem devoid of rational
purpose. At the same time, we find conflict unpleasant, stressful,
and noxious. We are torn by a magnet-like duality of attraction and
repulsion about conflict. Let's look more closely now at the more
positive pole of the magnet, the desire for peace.

Ambivalence

The desire for peace is a purely emotional experience, a felt need. On the strictly unemotional, rational level during arguments, we are also interested in achieving preferred solutions, in getting our way. The emotional and rational concerns must be compromised. We can seldom fully have both peace in the relationship and our preferred solution. The tension between these two desires is illustrated in the Conflict Ambivalence Grid*:

Figure 16:
Conflict Ambivalence Grid

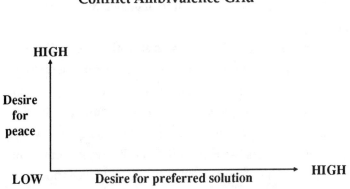

HIGH

Desire
for
peace

LOW   Desire for preferred solution   HIGH

Hard and Soft Bargainers

In attempting to reconcile this ambivalence, each person strikes an often uneasy balance between the two desires. Some of us care more strongly for one outcome than for the other. The relative strengths of these two desires determines how "hard" we are as bargainers.

---

*   Various two-dimensional grid models in conflict behavioral style analysis have been presented by Robert Blake and Jane Mouton, Alan Filley, Kenneth Thomas, and others.

The greater our desire for peace, the more likely we are to offer or welcome conciliatory gestures, including concessions on our preferred solution to the issue(s) being debated. If our desire for peace is low, then we are willing to sacrifice peacefulness in the relationship in order to maximize attainment of our preferred solution.

A person whose balance of desires is like this,

Figure 17:
Conflict Ambivalence Grid (hard bargainer).

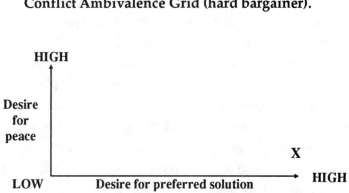

would be experienced by her Other as a "hard bargainer." A person whose balance of concerns is like this,

Figure 18:
Conflict Ambivalence Grid (soft bargainer).

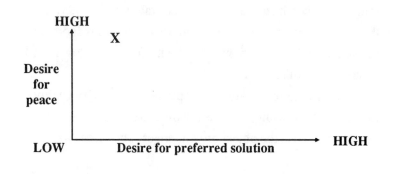

will sacrifice self-interest on substantive issues in order to maintain peaceful relations.

We differ from each other on the balance of these two desires, and our individual compromises between them may vary from situation to situation. Still, in any conflict, each of us is concerned about both keeping the relationship harmonious and getting what we want from solutions to the substantive issues. To the extent that desire for peace exists at all, it is a force toward conciliation.

Catharsis

Sigmund Freud was the most notable, but not the first, to advocate "the talking cure." He rediscovered what all of us experience from time to time in our daily lives: Simply talking about our troubles relaxes physical and emotional tension. "Supportive counseling" is little more than the talking cure packaged as weekly appointments with an empathetic listener. Counseling provides a regular opportunity for people to talk about their worries and problems with a good sounding board. This discharge of pent-up tension is called "catharsis."

Direct Aggression

How does catharsis help resolve interpersonal conflicts? No doubt you have discovered that when you are in conflict with someone, you can discharge some of the anger and tension by expressing it in ways other than direct face-to-face talking. Maybe you go to the gym for a vigorous game of squash, or you slam doors, or you talk to a friend. These are ways to drain off the overflow tension created by conflict.

But the long-term value of simply releasing angry energy is limited. In these examples, it is not discharged in the presence of the person who is the object of your anger. Therefore, you do not have the satisfaction of "direct aggression," of expressing your anger directly against its object. Rather, you are expressing it only toward a symbol of the object—the squash ball, the door, the mental image of your foe as you talk with the friend. By engaging only with the symbol of your Other, you are denied:

- The primal satisfaction of striking out (verbally, of course) against your foe, and

- The opportunity to hear and respond to your Other's responses and reactions that can lead to an exchange of conciliatory gestures.

Catharsis resulting simply from aggression toward a symbol provides a temporary release of tension. This is helpful as a means of managing the stress generated by conflict. Catharsis in combination with two-way live interaction with your Other also releases tension. More importantly, it occurs in a setting where conciliatory gestures can be responded to by either of you as they arise in conversation.

But a caution is in order. Catharsis is not always a good thing. Psychological research shows that face-to-face verbal aggression can actually increase tension and deepen conflict if done in an inappropriate context. The 4-Step Method, particularly the Cardinal Rules that outlaw Non-communication and Power-play throughout a Dialogue, provides insurance against harmful effects of catharsis.

Inhibitory Reflex in Territorial Behavior

Scientists who study the behavior of animals in their natural habitats (ethologists) have observed a pair of instincts that consistently control the behavior of two adult members of the same species during territorial encounters.

Aggression

The first instinct is aggression. Aggression occurs every time an animal perceives that another is violating a territorial boundary, or appears to have that intention. When a territorial violation occurs, the "home-turf" animal rushes to meet the intruder with threatening postures, and may physically attack unless the intruder immediately withdraws. Most conflicts between animals are resolved in this way—one individual retreats. It is this retreat from encounter that in modern human behavior, we have labeled the Wrong Reflex #1: Non-communication.

Sometimes, the intruder persists in attempting to take possession of the home-turf animal's territory. Then a fight occurs. But fights between animals in the wild hardly ever result in death. Why not? Because a second instinct prevents violence from escalating beyond an acceptable level, and serves as a mechanism for peaceful resolution.

This second instinct is the inhibitory reflex. We all have seen the inhibitory reflex happen, without paying much attention to it. Two dogs, Rex and Tiny, get into a territorial fight in one's yard. Tiny quickly recognizes the futility of fighting with the stronger Rex and rolls over, showing his soft belly. Rex, if he chose, could bite Tiny's belly and possibly kill him. But by rolling over (a conciliatory gesture), Tiny has elicited the inhibitory reflex in Rex. Rex is absolutely constrained by instinct from biting Tiny's tummy. Any sign of self-protective posturing by Tiny would release Rex from the inhibitory reflex's constraining muzzle, freeing him to bite.

So the picture is this: Tiny lies belly-up on the ground, his soft, vulnerable tummy exposed, whimpering nervously. Meanwhile, Rex is poised with perilous fangs hovering above the submissive

Tiny, growling menacingly. This scene continues a few moments, long enough for Rex to drive home his point that he is the winner. Rex then struts slowly away, the proud victor.

Tiny's conciliatory gesture automatically triggered Rex's inhibitory reflex, preventing dangerous escalation of the conflict. Where did Tiny's conciliatory gesture come from? Certainly Tiny could predict that to continue fighting would have dire consequences to his health. He probably knew it was an uphill battle before ever encountering Rex to start with. He is not blind; he could see Rex's superior size and strength. So why did Tiny get involved in this hopeless encounter?

Tiny and Rex have dog-versions of what we have called in this book emotional issues. Tiny made a show of confronting Rex because his self-esteem, his pride, required it. But Tiny is no fool. He did so "knowing" instinctively that he could trust Rex to inhibit his aggression as soon as he employed the conciliatory gesture trick. Tiny got his "day in court" with Rex without getting hurt. So, dogs and other animals are instinctively equipped with the "knowledge" of how to use the conciliatory gesture whenever it is needed to elicit the inhibitory reflex in others.

Among dogs, as well as in every other species of predatory social animal on earth, the conciliatory gesture automatically elicits the inhibitory reflex. This happens just as surely as the aggressive reflex is triggered when an intruder enters another's territory. So aggression and inhibition are the two instincts that control intra-species fights.

Inhibition in Humans

Now, what about us humans? We are not driven by instinct as absolutely as are animals. Still, we have evolved from common ancestors with other animals who share our planet today, and so we share an evolutionary heritage. We are different from animals in many ways; we are also similar to animals in some remarkable ways. The fact that the aggression and inhibitory reflexes are found throughout the animal world offers us an opportunity to learn something about how we handle human conflict by examining conflict between animals.

Before looking at how people follow a similar pattern in two-person conflicts, let's mention some differences between humans and animals that must be considered in drawing any parallels:

1) Having developed spoken language, we usually conduct our aggression via words rather than by physical attacks and attack posturing.

2) Our "territory" is often less concrete and geographical in nature, and more abstract and conceptual. Intruders in our homes and our offices, of course, arouse home-turf protective reactions. But so do co-workers who attempt to take over part of our job responsibilities, employees who overstep the bounds of their authority, managers who attempt to impose a sex-role stereotype on opposite-sex members of their staff, colleagues who do not acknowledge the privileges of our professional rank, and salespeople who insist on taking up our time. In these examples, our "territory" is not clearly delineated. These uncertain boundaries make it difficult to determine whether a trespass is accidental or intentional.

3) In most human territorial disputes, both participants often feel that they are on their own home turf and are simply protecting themselves from unwarranted intrusion by the

Other. So it is much less clear that one individual is "in the wrong" by knowingly violating boundaries. More often, both participants feel their rights are violated by the other.

4) We have more free will in controlling how we behave than do animals. That is, we can choose to act differently from how our emotions might propel us to act.

5) We live our daily lives in unnaturally large groups such as cities and megacorporations, requiring us to interact closely with people whom we do not know well enough to trust.

Natural Weapons

One additional difference between humans and animals is a key to understanding two-person conflicts: People do not have "natural weapons." Natural weapons, like sharp claws and long teeth, are parts of the body that could do physical damage to another in a physical fight. Every other predatory social animal has natural weapons—humans do not. We do, however, have vestiges of natural weapons, such as finger- and toe-nails and the "canine" teeth. These features of our bodies are puny remnants of what used to be, earlier in our evolutionary history, effective natural weapons that were used for preying on other animals for food and for sorting out the dominance hierarchy (the "pecking order") in our social groups. Over the past few million years, however, these body parts have become less useful and have physically diminished.

What purpose does the inhibitory reflex serve for animals? Why did it evolve in the first place? Clearly, if Tiny's conciliatory gesture did not cause Rex to back off, Rex could use his long sharp teeth and powerful jaws to kill Tiny—not as prey for food, but as a member of the same species with whom he is simply sorting out dominance. If the natural weapons that animals have for predation and food-acquisition were used without restraint, then the species would be less effective in reproducing and succeeding in its environment. The inhibitory reflex evolved in parallel with natural weapons as a behavioral mechanism to restrain their destructive use within social groups. So the combination of the aggressive impulse, along with the inhibitory reflex serves as a very effective behavioral mechanism in maintaining social order among animals.

Our Unreliable Inhibitory Reflex

Now let's look again at humans. As our natural weapons have become vestigial over the past several million years, the inhibitory reflex which had previously evolved to accompany them has also become vestigial. So, our inhibitory reflex is far weaker and less reliable than that of other animals. This would not present a problem except that over the past few thousand years (far too short a time for evolution to have brought adaptive changes) we have drastically changed the structure of social and community life. In early human social groupings, dominance had to be sorted out only in well-structured groups of a couple of dozen members, all of whom were born and reared together. When the group became larger than twenty or so, several members split off to form another group.

Today we live and work in "unnatural" social groupings. Organizations force people into ongoing, interdependent relationships. But co-workers did not grow up together and therefore did not learn at an early age to accept a position in the dominance hierarchy. Organizations are usually larger than the naturally occurring groups we evolved in, and for which our social behavioral mechanisms are adapted. Even the modern marriage may be an arrangement that is imposed on us by the demands of our exceedingly complex communities. Certainly the equal-status, shared-power marriage is a recent social invention that is more congruent with twentieth-century humanistic values than with social values of previous millennia.

Predicament of Modern Life

So, as the year 2000 approaches, we humans find ourselves in ongoing, interdependent relationships that we are not well-equipped through evolution to manage peacefully. Specifically, the threats to our "turf" at work arouse our self-defensive aggressive reflex, and we do not have a reliable behavioral mechanism to extricate ourselves from the retaliatory cycle once it begins. Using a conciliatory gesture no longer ensures an automatic inhibitory reflex from our Other. Since our conflicts normally take the form of verbal arguments, verbal conciliatory gestures are often not heard, or are misinterpreted as a deceptive, manipulative tactic. Even when a conciliatory gesture is heard, it can be taken as an opportunity to "go for the jugular" and win the fight.

The human inhibitory reflex is weak. But it does exist, and the modest automatic impulse that remains can be employed as the critically important fourth force for bringing harmony to two-person conflicts. It is the element in the 4-Step Method that triggers the Breakthrough that permits the negotiation of both-gain agreements. It is that gentle nudge to respond in kind when one says to us, "I'm sorry" or "I made a mistake."

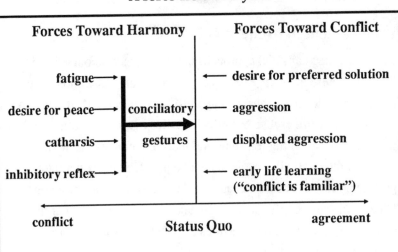

Figure 19:
A force-field analysis.

Forces Toward Harmony	Forces Toward Conflict

fatigue → | ← desire for preferred solution

desire for peace → conciliatory | ← aggression

catharsis → gestures | ← displaced aggression

inhibitory reflex → | ← early life learning ("conflict is familiar")

conflict   **Status Quo**   agreement

Explanation: Forces toward harmony push the status quo toward agreement, while other forces push toward continued conflict. The 4 Step Method, by enabling the forces toward harmony to occur during Dialogue, moves the status quo along the continuum from conflict to agreement.

HARMONIZING THE FORCES

Fatigue from sustained effort, desire for peaceful relationships, release of tension through catharsis, and the inhibitory reflex to conciliatory gestures are human experiences that are not limited only to the 4-Step Method. They occur constantly through daily living. The power of the 4-Step Method for managing differences lies in the harnessing of these forces to bring harmony to discordant relationships. The structure, context, rules, and tasks prescribed by the Method help these four psychological dynamics join together in producing that special window of opportunity for interpersonal peace—the Breakthrough.

Chapter 21:

A SUMMARY:
HOW THE 4-STEP METHOD TURNS
CONFLICT INTO COOPERATION

Finally, standing upon the behavioral science foundation laid in the previous two chapters, let's review the 4-Step Method, summarizing how each step contributes to transforming conflict into cooperation and builds interpersonal harmony.

Step 1: FIND A TIME TO TALK

Setting a time and the groundrules for having a conversation with your Other about the issues that concern you . . .

- Establishes communication, the most fundamental and essential requirement for mutually agreeable solutions.

- Establishes Cardinal Rule #1, which prevents the Wrong Reflex of Non-communication from blocking resolution by ensuring that both participants are present and actively involved.

- Establishes Cardinal Rule #2, which prevents the Wrong Reflex of Power-play from resulting in defeat of one participant, laying the basis for future deterioration of the relationship.

Step 2: PLAN THE CONTEXT

Preparing the time-and-place environment for your talk . . .

- Ensures steady progress through the confrontation phase of the Dialogue, ensuring that both participants complete the "journey to the top of the mountain."

- Ensures sufficient time for catharsis to occur during the confrontation phase so that genuine conciliatory gestures can emerge.

■ Protects the Dialogue from the interruptions and distractions that can cause your meeting to fail.

Step 3: TALK IT OUT

The *Opening* . . .

■ Establishes a climate of non-defensiveness and optimism.

■ Reaffirms commitment to the Cardinal Rules of engagement during the Dialogue.

■ Establishes an expectation that a both-gain solution will be found through joint searching.

The *Invitation* **launches the Dialogue.**

The *Dialogue* . . .

■ Empowers the initiator of this Method to guide communication with the Other to a constructive conclusion by performing:

Task #1: Staying engaged in the Essential Process, keeping participants in uninterrupted contact long enough for the four psychological forces to combine to produce conciliatory gestures; and

Task #2: Supporting the Other's conciliatory gestures, so that friendly comments will not be taken as opportunities to "score a point in the win-lose game" thereby sabotaging progress; leading to

. . .

The *Breakthrough*, in which both participants' attitudes shift from me-against-you to us-against-the-problem, a window of opportunity during which they can . . .

Step 4: MAKE A DEAL

Once Breakthrough occurs, framing a behaviorally specific agreement . . .

- Allows mutual consent to decisions that require consensus.

- Creates a mutually acceptable plan for activities that require participation by both people.

- Ensures a balanced give-and-take that provides an incentive for each participant to fulfill her obligations in the agreement.

- Enhances interpersonal trust.

- Provides an experience in successfully getting around the "boulder in the road," increasing participants' optimism about their ability to manage their differences and resolve disputed issues in the future.

Appendix 1:
NOTES FOR THE OTHER

[From *Talk It Out! 4 Steps to Managing People Problems in Your Organization* by Daniel Dana (Amherst, Massachusetts: HRD Press, 1990). This appendix may be reproduced without restriction.]

I am asking you to join with me in searching for mutually acceptable solutions to certain issues that we disagree about, and work with me to build a better relationship between us.

This process requires that we find a time to talk without interruption until we are able to find some agreement. In order for this discussion to be successful, both of us must accept two "Cardinal Rules."

Cardinal Rule #1: DO NOT WITHDRAW from communication, whether from frustration and hopelessness, or as a retaliatory action.

This means we cannot walk out, give up, or stop trying until some kind of agreement is reached. Let's agree to accept feeling frustrated and angry during our talk, if necessary, and to persevere even if we want to quit.

Cardinal Rule #2: DO NOT USE POWER-PLAYS to "win" a power struggle between us by defeating the Other with threats, ultimatums, or force.

This means that any solution that involves either of us being involuntarily forced to accept the other's demands is not acceptable. We must continue to search for a solution to which we both can agree and from which we both can gain.

If the subject of our dispute involves a decision to which we both must consent, or an activity in which we both must participate, we must reach an agreement. Good agreements are:

- Behaviorally specific, meaning that we will discuss in detail WHO, is to do WHAT, by WHEN, for HOW LONG, under what CONDITIONS, etc.

- Balanced, so that each of us will feel that the agreement is fair.

- Written, to help us remember the details of our agreement in the future.

Thanks for caring enough about our relationship to work with me on this.

Appendix 2:

HOW TO USE THIS BOOK FOR QUICK REFERENCE

This book may look like many others, to be read from start to finish, then to be put on your bookshelf to gather dust.

But this is designed so you can use it as a reference book, more like a dictionary, almanac, or thesaurus. First, read it through once, cover to cover, to familiarize yourself with the 4-Step Method and how it works. Then keep this with your other reference books—on your desk or a nearby bookshelf.

Everyone encounters a conflict from time to time in important relationships. Each time you do, reach for this resource. After you have read it once, here is how to use this book:

A. Refresh your understanding of the 4-Step Method by reviewing Chapter 7: A Skeleton View.

B. Ask yourself this question:

"Do I feel comfortable using the Method to resolve this conflict?"

C. If you answer yes, go to step D below.

If you answer no, look through the following possible concerns to more clearly identify the reasons for your discomfort:

I'm not sure it will work.

I don't know if the Other will do it.

I feel awkward suggesting we have a meeting.

I don't want to be the one who initiates it, to seem like I'm giving in.

I can't trust the other person to not use unfair power advantage. I am too vulnerable to being punished.

The conflict/relationship/issue is not important enough to me to go through the trouble and discomfort of talking about it.

I think my conflict is more of a crisis than the 4-Step Method is designed to deal with.

I might get too nervous to do it right.

I'm concerned that the Other is not strong enough.

I don't have the time to deal with it.

I don't want the Other to get upset.

It's easier just to keep things the way they are now.

I don't think the Other would understand what to do.

I'm afraid I would just give in to the Other's pressure.

I would get too angry.

I know the Other will not change; it would just be wasted effort.

Your concerns probably fall into any of five categories. Review the suggested sections of the book to explore your questions:

1) Concerns about importance of the problem
   See Chapter 1.
2) Concerns about appropriateness of the problem
   See Chapters 5 and 17.
3) Concerns about whether the 4-Step Method can solve the problem
   See Chapters 16 and 17, and Part 4.
4) Concerns about yourself (confidence in your ability to use the Method)
   See Chapters 11 and 12.

5) Concerns about your Other's ability or willingness to participate in the Method

    See Chapters 9 and 17.

D. Answer this question:

    "After reviewing the relevant information in this book, am I confident that the 4-Step Method is designed to resolve conflicts of the kind I am concerned with?"

    (Note: Do not expect yourself to be entirely free of apprehension. Review the discussion about discomfort in Chapter 15 if you are tempted to avoid a Dialogue with your Other as the Method prescribes.)

E. If your answer is yes, do it. Use the checklist on page 211 to be sure you're fully prepared.
    If your answer is no, look at alternative recommendations in Chapters 5 and 17.

F. Congratulate yourself for being a problem-solver, not a problem-avoider!

CHECKLIST
Before starting,

_____ Review "How to Use This Book for Quick Reference" (Appendix 2) to be sure the solution fits the problem.

_____ Review the 4-Step Method (Chapter 7).

Before Step 3 ("Talk It Out"), be sure you've covered the following:

_____ Both schedules cleared for adequate time period?

_____ Interruptions prevented (phone or walk-ins)?

_____ No distractions (seating comfort, visual movement, sound, thirst, temperature, etc.)?

_____ Both agree to stay until agreement is reached?

_____ Both agree to talk about the issues (Cardinal Rule #1)?

_____ Both agree to not use Power-Play to defeat the other (Cardinal Rule #2)?

_____ Do you have the Essential Process clearly in mind?

OK, do it.

GLOSSARY

4-Step Method A behaviorally specific procedure for managing differences between people in ongoing, interdependent, two-person relationships.

Aggression Behavior that is intended by its exhibitor to harm the interests of its target.

Ambivalence The co-existence of opposing or incompatible attitudes, needs, or interests in the same individual.

Assertion Behavior that insists on one's own rights without violating the rights of others.

Bad-Person Illusion The perceptual phenomenon of erroneously attributing the cause of an interpersonal conflict to the defective personal characteristics of the Other.

Blips Conflicts of minor importance that are resolved or disappear spontaneously. (Level 1 conflicts)

Both-gain An attitudinal and behavioral stance by a person in conflict in which the possibility of mutually beneficial outcomes is assumed.

Boulder-in-the-Road Illusion The phenomenon of erroneously perceiving impossibility of resolving a conflict.

Breakthrough The occurrence during face-to-face issue-focused dialogue of a mutual shift of attitude by both partners from "me-against-you" to "us-against-the-problem."

Cardinal Rules Guidelines for engaging in communication with others that prevent behaviors that manifest the "wrong reflexes."

Clashes Conflicts that, if disregarded, impair the capacity of relationships to satisfy the needs of its partners. (Level 2 conflicts)

Cognitive Dissonance The inherently uncomfortable experience of two or more mental events (beliefs, attitudes, values, perceptions) that are incompatible with each other.

Conciliatory Gestures Uncoerced behaviors, typically verbal, that display vulnerability to one's opponent in conflict.

Conflict A condition between two interdependent people in which one or both feel angry at the other and perceive the other as being at fault.

Crises Conflicts that threaten the continuation of a relationship. (Level 3 conflicts)

Deal The balanced, behaviorally specific, written agreement that is reached as a result of using the 4-Step Method.

Dialogue The face-to-face, issue-focused verbal communication that occurs during step 3 of the 4-Step Method.

Difference A state of disparity in needs, values, attitudes, goals, or self-interests between two individuals in an ongoing, interdependent relationship.

Emotional Issues Matters of concern to persons in conflict that represent the psychological needs whose satisfaction is sought in the relationship.

Essential Process Face-to-face talking between two people about the issues on which they differ without interruption for as long as necessary to reach the Breakthrough.

Inhibitory Reflex The instinctive response to a conciliatory gesture displayed by an opponent in conflict, resulting in termination or suspension of aggressive behavior.

Interpersonal Pertaining to two individuals.

Issues Matters of concern to persons in conflict on which incompatible positions are held. (See Emotional, Pseudo- substantive, Substantive.)

Mediation The role of a neutral third party in facilitating the search for mutually acceptable, self-determined agreements between disputants.

Negotiation The process of searching for agreement between people who have apparently different self-interests.

Non-communication The behavioral strategy for coping with interpersonal conflict involving withdrawal from face-to-face conversation. (Wrong Reflex #1)

Other One's partner in an ongoing, interdependent, two-person relationship.

Polarization The tendency toward defining opposite positions on issues in conflict.

Position The preferred solution to a disputed issue that is put forth by a party in conflict.

Power-play The behavioral strategy for coping with interpersonal conflict involving the exercise or threat of force to overwhelm the resistance put forth by the Other. (Wrong Reflex #2)

Projection The process of attributing to the Other one's unwanted feelings, attitudes, values, and beliefs that are incompatible with other such feelings, thereby resolving one's intrapsychic ambivalence about a disputed issue.

Pseudo-substantive Issues Matters of concern to persons in conflict that are consciously or unconsciously represented falsely as substantive issues, but are in fact wholly or partially manifestations of emotional issues.

Retaliatory Cycle An iterative process in which two persons in conflict engage in mutual retribution and defensive counter-attack.

Submission Behavior that allows another person to violate one's rights.

Substantive Issues Matters of concern that accurately represent the objective self-interest of the person.

Win-Lose Illusion The phenomenon of erroneously or prematurely assuming that no both-gain outcome is possible.

Wrong Reflexes Automatic attitudinal and behavioral responses to conflict that derive from the "fight" and "flight" impulses. (See Non-communication and Power-play.)

INDEX

supportive counseling, 186
synergy, 30, 85

unmanaged employee conflict, 9
uncoerced behaviors, 80
unconscious hostility, 11
United States Congress, 18
unpleasant encounter, 67
us-against-the-problem, 92, 99,
    179, 198

verbal conciliatory gestures, 193

win-lose conclusion, 68
win-lose conflict, 44, 172
Win-Lose Illusion, 29-30, 86, 216
win-lose power struggle, 91
win-lose situations, 30
workplace conflicts, 3, 13
Wrong Reflexes, 25, 26, 28, 31,
    34, 35, 40, 44, 54, 63, 67, 84,
    86, 89, 130, 137, 216

Zen, 121

ABOUT THE AUTHOR

A pioneer in the field of conflict resolution, Dan Dana is internationally recognized as the originator of Managerial Mediation. Holding the Ph.D. in psychology, Dr. Dana has served on the faculty of several universities in the United States, and has been guest lecturer at institutions in Holland, Sweden, England, Turkey, and Hong Kong. His warm, engaging speaking style, accompanied by his depth of knowledge, makes him a favorite with corporate and public audiences alike.

The founder and Executive Director of Mediation Training Institute International, Dr. Dana maintains a limited consulting practice dedicated to solving problems through the technologies of managing difference. In this book, he offers the lay reader a practical guide for using this technology in everyday worklife.

Dr. Dana welcomes readers' comments and inquiries. He may be reached at PO Box 6261, Wolcott, Connecticut 06716 USA.